P9-CKA-703

ROME
from the air

173384 9

14.95

This book is dedicated to Gisella

Pages 4–5: It took exactly one year for builders under Hadrian's orders to raise up the eight spans of the Ponte Sant'Angelo. It was Pope Gregory I who gave this bridge its name, after a reputed appearance of an angel on the top of the nearby castle. In 1450, the original bridge collapsed and was rebuilt: all but two of the ten angels on the present bridge are signed by Gianlorenzo Bernini.

Rome from the Air

Translated from Italian by David Bloom

© Times Editions 1988
1 New Industrial Road, Singapore 1953

First published in the United States of America in 1989 by
Rizzoli International Publications, Inc.
597 Fifth Avenue, New York, NY 10017

All rights reserved. No part of this publication may be reproduced, stored in a retrieval system or transmitted in any form, or by any means, electronic, mechanical or otherwise, without the prior permission in writing of the copyright holder.

Printed by Tien Wah Press, Singapore
Colour separation by Far East Offset, Malaysia
Typeset by Superskill Graphics, Singapore

Library of Congress Cataloging-in-Publication Data

Rossi, Guido A., 1949–
    [Roma dal Cielo. English]
    Rome from the air / Guido A. Rossi and Franco Lefèvre.
    Translation of : Roma dal Cielo.
    ISBN 0-8478-1017-8
    1. Rome (Italy) — Description — 1975–   — Views. 2. Rome (Italy) —
    Aerial photographs.   I. Lefèvre, Franco, 1926–   .   II. Title.
    DG806.8.R6713 1989
    914.5'632'00222 — dc1

                             88-28658
ISBN 0-8478-1017-8   CIP

ROME
from the air

Photographed by Guido Alberto Rossi
Text by Franco Lefèvre

RIZZOLI
NEW YORK

Contents

CITY ON THE TIBER
page fifteen

ANCIENT PLEASURES
page twenty-seven

THE IDEAL CITY
page forty-nine

TWO ARTISTS, ONE STYLE
page sixty-seven

THE *DOLCE VITA*
page one hundred and nine

Index
page one hundred and forty-three

Acknowledgements
page one hundred and forty-four

This is the Porta del Popolo where, from ancient times up to the nineteenth century, crowds of artists, the hungry poor, conquerors, and pilgrims gathered to ask permission to enter Rome; and so do we now, but with a difference: this time the pilgrim has abandoned the pavement and chosen the route of the sky …

A magically unexpected perspective, the heart of Rome harmoniously includes in its spendour old roofs, belltowers and domes (that of the Pantheon emerges in the centre). The view is dominated from the back by two antithetical masses — the Colosseum and the Vittoriano.
Pages 10–11: The Vatican basks in the glow of sunset.
Pages 12–13: The palette-knife colours of the sky hypnotize visitors into what modern Roman poet Trilussa has called "beflagging their hearts".

CITY ON THE TIBER

Goethe was right: "Here in Rome, the current drags us along, as soon as we have put one foot in the boat." Two centuries have passed, and yet this cursory-sounding sentence of the great writer from Frankfurt still seems definitive, downright unquestionable. Better than mere language, the images in this book say the same thing again, so palpably emotive are they, so entirely inside the discourse between city and citizen — in short, so authentically Roman. The very side-slips and nose dives of Guido Alberto Rossi's helicopter look as if they had been inspired by the aphorism — in its dry delicacy like a Dantean judgment. From the air as well as on land, one gets that impression of being dragged along by the city. And so we too are about to put a foot into the boat: this time armed with a camera lense. And the lense is the liberator of our invincible curiosity, free from the distracted pause and flight of rhetoric, making no concessions to the improbable flavours of the tourist's deja vu.

Here she is beneath us, Rome the masterful, Rome the maternal, the epigone of a metropolis weighed down under the experience of more than twenty-seven centuries. Unimaginably sinuous, crisscrossed by hundreds upon hundreds of alleys and tiny squares, voluptuous, ironical, blasphemous, and generous, tipping us the wink and at the same time capable of unpredictable blushes; the Grande Signora leers from her roof tops and fountains, communicates the complete register of her feelings in a vast reverberating murmur. She has a reputation for mockery, and when she offers us umpteen little corners that have never been catalogued, she is laughing at us. This self-directed irony is like a game between Rome and her children. We are still being pulled along.

The gentle interplay of paths starts from a fixed origin, and that is the Tiber, which drags us along as if in a drunken time machine, in an ungentle interplay of historical moments. The connective tissue of Rome — in space, in time, in the organization of its social world — draws its strength from the river and its sly meandering. From the time of the mythical founders of the city, Romulus and Remus (before they were weaned, the Tiber current carried them off in a wicker basket and landed them at the feet of the shepherd Faustolus, in the small valley where the Forum was to be built), until the nineteenth century, this lazy, untrustworthy stream, grumbling and intrusive, has had an almost exclusive sway over the

destiny of the inhabitants — not to mention their precariously-built homes. Ugo Martegani and Vann Ronsisvalle document the unruly reign of the Tiber in their book, *Rome, the Devil and the Holy Water*:

"The site of Rome, the womb from which it was born, was one big swamp, from Ponte Milvio to the Aventine Hill, miserable to look at and unhealthy. Even in the times of the Borgia, stagnant water lapped the sides of the Palatine; and when Lucrezia Borgia fled the dangerous splendour of the papal court, after her acrimonious divorce from the Duke of Pesaro, she rode with her little escort to the Dominican convent, San Sisto, on the road to the Baths of Caracalla. Noble ladies in retreat there found death by malaria a greater threat than poison. Nor were things any better in the heart of town, considering that Montaigne could not count on leaving his rooms at the Hostria dall'Orso other than by boat. He, with all his ailments, was often confined by the whims of the Tiber which chose exactly that point to break out to the valley as far as the Jewish ghetto."

More like a neurotic delta than a regular and reliable waterway, the Tiber has always meant (since the first faint gleams of the city's origins as a few miserable huts dispersed in the deadly marsh) the curse of unpredictable catastrophe. The most fitting comparison would be with the Aeolian volcanoes or Mt. Vesuvius: those fearful eruptions are beyond imagining, but neither does flood water brook any appeal; it flows, insinuating and unrelenting, like lava. Visitors to the city are certain to notice high water inscriptions on the walls of many a palace and many a church in Rome's historic centre. The threatening water levels have, over the centuries, been like the predations of an invading army. In fact, the most memorable of the last floodings dates back to December 1870, only two months after the Savoyard army invaded and occupied Rome.

And yet, as malevolent and destructive as this river can be, it has earned its honourific of sacred river, down the years. Urban planners of the last century tried to heighten the Tiber's sanctity, but their pomposity was misguided; they tried to create setpieces which showed a river in procession through its banks. It is true that Rome is divided in two by this river, but it is also caressed by its delicate design; the city shows off its captivating charm best just where the Tiber effaces itself, putting on a severely poor and humble look, and at the same time letting itself go consciously slack.

An incredibly geometric order in a city that has always been given to curvilinear improvisation, this is a bit of urban-planning reality joining the old Piazza del Trullo (now Piazza del Popolo) to Piazza Venezia across Via del Corso. As Charles de Brosses wrote in his Lettres familières écrites d'Italie: *"Nothing in Piazza del Popolo gives the magnificent impression of Rome better than this initial view, which strikes the visitor at the moment of arrival."*

A close and conspiratorial huddle of tiny terraces with a domesticated air alternates with the bizarre belvederes of artists, mostly foreigners, to make up the skyline of a quarter that, rising from Via Condotti, Via Borgognona, Via Frattina, Via del Babuino to Trinità de' Monti (in the centre), has looked at street-level for the last two centuries like one long shopwindow.

From these points the memories begin — where legends mix with fact, where purely mythological characters are confused with those personages who not only existed, but left behind them signs to prove it.

The Latins and the Sabines were the first tribes to settle in Latium, Rome's district, now called Lazio, probably between the ninth and tenth century BC, on the Palatine, the Viminal, and the Quirinal hills. They began trade on the Tiber, and so a city grew. This led to the reign of the seven Etruscan kings of Rome, and the foundation of the metropolis — called Ruma around the first half of the sixth century BC. The birth of the Republic came after the overthrow of the last of the seven kings, the fabled Tarquin the Proud, in 509 BC.

The greatest trade activity was concentrated in the Forum in its north-facing parts, the Comitium and the Basilica Porcia. Plautus left a record of the Forum's comings and goings during his time (the second century BC): "If you want to see a man breaking his word, go to the Comitium; rich husbands that want to ruin themselves are to be found by the Basilica; that's where there are as well trollops, perverts, and people trying to make good on contracts; you'll see those that love to dine in town with friends at the fish market."

Another realistic account of those who haunted the Forum was written by the master of the epigram, Martial in AD 85. "Chloë, that wicked woman, wrote on the tombs of her seven husbands: 'This was my work.' Who in the Forum would dare to be more explicit than this?"

These characters, and their stories, should be elaborated in the theatre, or the opera, yet these brief brushstrokes still produce a powerful effect. We owe a debt to these poets as well as to the artists and builders of that epoch. The human fresco of their writings documents old Rome in a way that is often superior to all the voluted capitals and mosaic tesserae that have been unearthed under the Palatine hill. This debt should also be extended to the story-tellers and historians of later centuries.

But before we attend to them, we must first say farewell to the Forum, and to that squat stone pillar, the Miliarum Aureum or Golden Milepost, that the Emperor Augustus set up in its centre. The pillar and its attendant stones, the *raggiera*, were considered the centre to which all of the roads of the Roman Empire ran, from all the most remote corners of the world; for, by the time of Augustus, Rome had grown in leaps and bounds.

And with the city, so grew the importance of the Tiber. In the first centuries to follow, the river became more and more a part of everyday life; it was virtually the only route by which building materials could be carried to the massive construction sites. Today no trace is left of the Marmorata port (also called Porto di Ripa Grande — it was near Porta Portese) where the marble and breccia were unloaded, soon to form the foundations as well as the glitter of the homes of the most influential families. Stone, timber and mortar, needless to say, were also sought after. But all this dealing could not detach the Romans from their regard for tradition, and the centre of Rome never moved far from its roots in the soil, the so-called "furrows of Romolus".

The origins were there, in the marshy valley that came to be known as the Forum. It was there that the first shepherds grazed their herds and lived off scarce grain and bony river fish. There is where the eventual Roman establishment would come from, the centre of the Septimontium, the famous seven hills, and the focus around which the perimeter of the city was measured — totalling some twenty kilometres during the reign of Constantine.

Although only fragments remain of the once-glorious Roman Imperial architecture, there are enough to stimulate some imagination, some mnemomic games, so let us try and visualize the scope of Rome, as a report from 354 BC suggests it: 37 gates, 11 aqueducts and 11 baths, eight bridges, two *campidogli*, 190 granaries, 11 forums, 36 marble arches, 1,152 fountains, two grand circuses, two amphitheatres, three theatres, ten basilicas, 254 mills, two great food markets, almost 2,000 residential homes, 80 gilt statues and 77 of ivory, and six obelisks. An orgy of stone, marble, precious metals, and multi-coloured ceramics, that threatened to satiate a population that fluctuated, according to contemporary sources, between 1,700,000 and two million.

Turning back upriver along the course of Father Tiber, under the cover of night we can approach the soldiers' barracks, or the little windows of rickety huts reflected in this torpid-looking, but sometimes capricious water. Then, discreetly, but keeping our eyes and ears at their sharpest, we can proceed into the narrow little streets, into the taverns and the shops.

And here one needs to know how to listen, yes, listen to whispered voices bringing their stories and secrets across the long centuries — like those of the Christians.

There, in a part of Rome where the chic houses and sports clubs clash with the ancient woods of the hill of Saxa Rubra, on Via Flaminia, that was where Constantine won the decisive battle in 312 BC against his rival, Maxentius. Christianity found its great protector in Constantine, who enabled the followers of the Nazarene to practise their cult openly for the first time. Just a short time ago, as time is reckoned in Rome, the Christians took refuge from Roman power in narrow catacombs underground, and there gathered with their dead. They covered the walls with astonishing images, still admirable today. San Sebastiano, San Callisto on the Via Appia Antica, San Pancrazio on the Via Aurelia, the Domitilla on the Ardeatina, and the Priscilla on the Salaria are the catacombs that bear clearest witness to the time of Nero's fire, when the Christians lived with unspeakable persecutions.

In the meantime, up at ground level, Rome continued to burn. The ashes and the ruins formed a stratum of earth, metres thick, which was later to be covered with other buildings and temples. This is how the lower-lying parts of the city were uplifted to a remarkable extent. It is a piece of good luck for our present-day archeologists, it may be added, since from this underground has emerged the most persuasive evidence on the history and culture of Rome. Even the foundations of the baths, where rested those who cultivated the ideal of *otium cum dignitate* (dignified sloth), have left vestiges of an earlier civilization. It could be said that just as with New York City today, the building of a metropolis in those times was conceived of as a constant renewal, and it seemed only natural to build structures on the site where an analogous structure had been before.

"*Roma caput mundi*" was doubtless the city's inevitable destiny, but Rome was also its own *caput*, "head", in addition to being that of the world, and a distinctly hairy one it was at that. The architectural principle at work must have come from the need to maintain the position of the core citizenry, and the machinery of its political and commercial infrastructure. This explains why the city was so full of temples and why, in its height of splendour, it was filled with more tributes of praise than were ever found in the East: the forums of Augustus, of Nerva, of Vespasian and of Tarjan. Rather than compete with the glory of the city centre, Julius Caesar preferred living in the *suburba*, and the rich Mecenate chose a working-class neighbourhood on the Esquiline hill to build his villa.

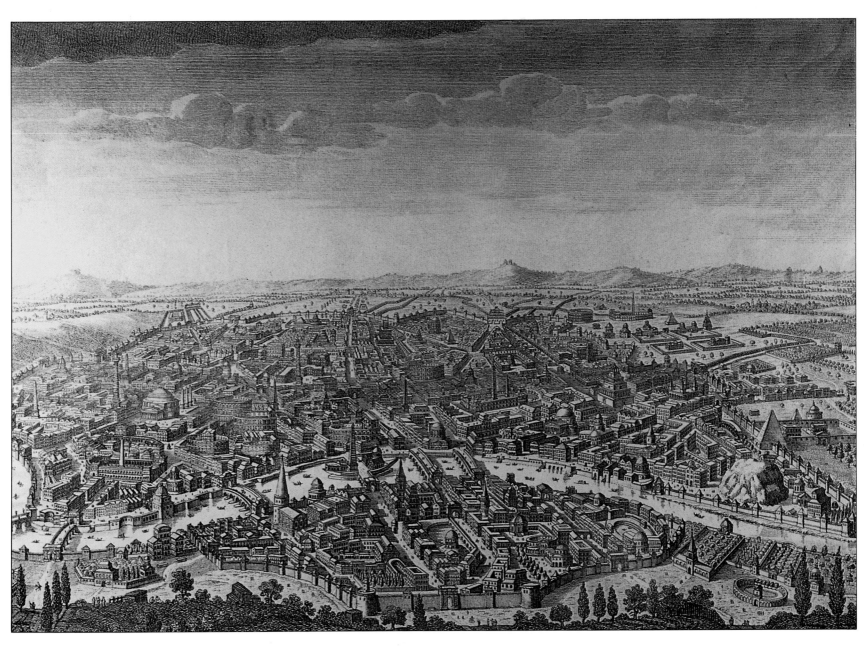

*The sometimes confused evidence of the fifteenth century engravers makes it clear that
in spite of invasions, Rome had succeeded in preserving some important traces of its
imperial times, such as the obelisks — this one is in the Tiberina isle.*

A few centuries later, all this changed. The citizens of this later age were inspired by one thing and one thing only: the devastation of ancient Rome. Although the sacking of Rome (still loaded with marvels, if only semi-inhabited, with fewer than a hundred thousand citizens) was ordered for 24 August 410 by Alaric, the champion pirates in this case were the Romans themselves.

Alaric's Visigoths put their hearts into destroying as many of Rome's prestigious homes as they could. In only three days, on the Aventine hill — the most aristocratic and richest of Rome — 130 mansions were pillaged and destroyed. Some years later, the Vandals of Genseric did the same, with the spoiling the Palace of the Caesars, the looting of the gold and precious stones of the Church and the Temple of Jove Optimus Maximus as well. The problem remains: how does one account for the rise of the great villas of Rome's feudal families, the Conti, the Colonna, the Barberini, the Savelli, the Crescenzi, and the Mellini? All of them systematically built towers and private homes using the marble and bronze stolen from the city. And the clergy and the everyday Romans looted too. Churches and commercial stalls were spangled with fragments of art, and monumental blocks of stone were ground for lime. And the things which had been spared from these carpet demolitions, especially the marble, were scattered across orchards and placed in courtyards, shown off to satisfy a misplaced concept of awe. "Leave the stones there, like the leftovers of a grand dinner party" wrote Ennio Flaiano in 1961, the most intelligent critic of today's city and author of *A Martian in Rome*.

Those dark years of pillage were inevitably the worst years of chaos in the city — a reflection of political and religious disorder. This progressive decline reached its nadir during the so-called Iron Age of the papacy, when it was at the total mercy of the Roman nobility. These satraps lacerated the city for eighty years, from AD 887 to 963, squabbling over the prize of naming their preferred popes. In fact, during that period there were 24 popes, one of them being the eleven-year-old Pope John XI, the son of the terrible Marozia and Sergius III. The fresco of Roman life took on even gloomier hues, and among the screams of war, nothing remained of the old certainty of law or the antique pride of being able to say one had been born a Roman. Nor did the processions of the Jubilees bring back any light, or the ceremonial visits by powerful admirers of the city still known as eternal. Instead, pesti-

lence haunted the city with genocide on either side of the Tiber. By then there were only a few thousand inhabitants, and we would have seen them as villagers in an extraordinarily diluted city. The city had become as elusive as a *fata morgana*. Rome, with the help of its solemn river, had taken on the image of something mummified, universally immutable, confined within the dusty and indefinable echoes of legend, forever, with no hope of repreive.

This new face that Rome adopted — doubtlessly the most sordid — would remain for a long time. Cruel battles raged between powerful patrician groups, the last versions of Oriental satraps and the representatives of the Church each vying for a new alliance. Yet the city seemed to possess a secret remedy: a natural solution that simply came with the next day finding its way through the darkness of the night. This remedy carried one name: imperturbability. A condition of the soul, in this case a collective unconscious, it seems to occur in historical cycles, as a byproduct of that bloodless skepticism of which Romans are always being accused.

Although not inclined to high-powered enterprise (for that too is a legendary characteristic of the Roman) the population had nothing against novelty itself, especially when it involved big institutions. This explains their loyalty to Alberic, another son of Marozia, who wiped out the temporal power of the popes with a single blow in 932, forming the new Republic, becoming its prince and reestablishing order in the city. He did this by entrusting twelve militia with the control of twelve districts, setting up lay justice in the place of ecclesiastic courts, and bringing even clerics to trial. In one thunderflash there was a return to the principle of the people's rule, the absolute antithesis of papal power. This about-face, at this point in time, made it seem as if the city was preparing for the overwhelming changes about to take place in the Renaissance and later in the Baroque period. Even the Medieval Church, with its measured severity, seemed to understand the need of the people to regain what had been lost — order and peace within the soul.

Beginning with Eugenius IV, pope from 1431 to 1447, the great push for the architectural renewal of the city began. Not without — it is worth noting — damaging the ancient buildings. Since everyone used the same method for reconstruction, no scandal arose. Popes, noblemen, and cardinals designed buildings only after they had first seen how much stone was available from the *pietraia*, the

This shows part of the model built for the army of General Nicolas Charles Oudinot when they beseiged Rome in 1849 to quell the Revolution for a unified Italy. To the left of Tiberina isle in its bend in the Tiber, is the Ghetto; to the right is Trastevere.

Rome 1941: just a few months after the outbreak of war, a support craft with the insignia of the Sovereign Military Order of Malta flies over Piazza Venezia before landing at the city airport in Via Salaria. At six in the morning the centre of Rome looks abandoned, the Vittoriano is on the left, and in the middle distance is the Theatre of Marcellus, with Trastevere in the background.

stone-source, by which they meant any classical building. They worked by removing the stone needed, anything from limestone to precious marble used in decoration. These "marble hunters" worked with official support. A document of 1452 tells us that a contracter named Giovanni Paglia Lombardo was given the right to transport 2,522 carts of travertine from the Colosseum for a period of nine months. The same thing happened to the Circus Maximus, the Curia, the Temple of the Vesta, the Temple of Venus and the basilica of Maxentius — just to name a few. All were used as open pit mines. It must be said, however, that from this destruction well-known, admirable buildings were created: Palazzo San Marco in Piazza Venezia, the churches of Santa Maria del Popolo, San Pietro in Montorio, Sant'Agostino, Santa Maria del Pace, the Santo Spirito Hospital.

It was during these years — working at lightning speed — that Baccio Pontelli and Donato Bramante left their artistic mark by turning Rome upside down. Under their tutelage, Rome seemed to fall in love with long straight lines, and more straight lines did they build, until in a few years she had forgotten the twists of her old alleys.

Here was a new way of seeing the city, a new ideological conception that turned her into a theatre of power. Here was created a new spatial Rome, a Rome once again the universal home, the centre in the political arena. All the madly triumphal architecture sponsored by the throne of Saint Peter was to culminate with the grandeur of St. Peter's basilica. Manlio Lupinacci puts it in perspective: "The planetary system of the domes that circle round the cupola divina, the divine dome, tries to be worthy of such majesty, by coming together in both harmony and grace.

"It is to a sort of triumphant corruption that we owe the obelisks that stand at the ends of the noble streets, to it we owe the Trevi Fountain, the solemnity of Piazza di Spagna and the famous steps to the Trinità de' Monti, and Piazza Navona with its fountains. But most of all, we owe our gratitude for the opportunity given to the artists of the day to develop their genius in the arts: in architecture, sculpture and painting.

"It is to nepotism that we owe the buildings of the Roman princes with their works of art and museums, buildings that in any other city would have been reserved for kings. If the reconstruction of St. Peter's, replacing the dilapidated basilica where Charlemagne was crowned, gave rise to the scandal of the Church's sale of indulgences;

even if all those princely residences were shrouded in intrigue, favouritism, and a carefree style of funding based on the irresponsibility of Cardinal-nephews and a munificence abstracted from the Papal Treasury, what can be done about it now? Anyone today who walks through Rome should admire Bernini's columns in St. Peter's Square and the facade of Palazzo Barberini, leaving thoughts of morality to some other time and place."

The time when great architecture, painting and sculpture fanned over the city came to a halt after the end of the blazing years of the Baroque, the years of Bernini and Borromini, who dominated that epoch and created a common language between sculpture and architecture.

From that time on, Rome seemed to have lost her thirst for renovation, being altogether sated with the passion of having great artists adorn the city. For more than two centuries to come the city seemed preoccupied with playing a kind of mirror-game, recapturing a self-image of Rome as the "rustic metropolis" (as Silvio Negro called it), overflowing with extraordinary contrasts.

Renaissance churches stood here and there among fallow fields full of ruins, or between vineyards, orchards and opulent villas. Flocks of goats and sheep still made themselves at home in the Forum near herds of moon-horned cattle, just as they were during the days of the Arcadian shepherd Evander; prickly shrubs and wild flowers thrived at the Colosseum growing more abundantly near the top.

This was the Rome that so astounded Goethe, Chateaubriand, Stendhal, Keats and the other great travellers of the eighteenth and nineteenth centuries. They all took up the habit of immersing themselves in those objects from the precious past which still survived: in all the emerging signs of Romanitas. These fine souls, these insatiable worshippers of a bygone age, used to love crossing the paths of people born in Borgo and in Trastevere ai Monti, who were believed to be the descendants of ancient Romans. As they approached, the foreigners carefully scrutinized Roman gestures and listened closely to their words in the hope of hearing revealed some true residuum of classic civilization. Even their clothing might tell something of the ancestors. Above all, foreigners were fascinated by the Roman dialect, uncorrupted as it is — that "Romansh" that was used to such great effect by the nineteenth-century Roman satirist and poet Giuseppe Gioacchino Belli. "This speech jumbles the different

classes of the entire people together". The way to understand the "Roman Romans" is to analyze the roots of the characteristic Roman cadence and the enormous repertoire of banter that they use.

Two definitions of the Roman people seem to hit their target best. According to Edmond About:

"Many are too proud to ask for a little money, but none are rich enough to turn it down; fanatical in loyalty and in hatred, easily moved but not easily convinced, temperate by habit but terrifying when drunk, these good devils — simple-hearted family people — are nevertheless sure of their superiority over other men."

Oreste Ciabattoni wrote more epigrammatically that "The primary characteristic of Romans is a weariness augmented by imagination."

It might seem that such a quarrelsome people would be incapable of generous gestures and yet as one of their favourite proverbs says: "Rome has never been a step-mother to anyone." The whole world is taken in here, completely, no matter what station in life, as long as arrogance or overwheening pride are left behind by those who land on the banks of the Tiber.

Today within a multiform Rome, more than two thirds of it rebuilt in modern style, a Rome that has attained a stable population of around four million people, a Rome that since 1870 has played host to the greatest of real estate speculators, Monsignor de Merode being in the lead, it is still possible to find yourself rapt by the wonder of ancient stones, by the Renaissance buildings and by the churches from so many ages — even from the time when Rome had no more than 20,000 inhabitants.

But if you want to sink into this sensation, if you want to give in to it entirely, a word of warning: Rome is to be seen and sipped in the forbidden hours, as loving the city is best as a secret passion — at dawn or during the night, when the noise of the traffic is stilled, and when the fountains bubble and sing to each other in the small squares and dubious side streets of the city. For those who want to remove themselves from the undifferentiated collective unconsciousness and who consider themselves individual enough for a Rome that once was, only in these precious moments is it permitted to listen to the voices, sumptuous, humble, muffled, musical, mocking and sombre, of so many ages past.

It is with the affectionate help of these whispers that we we always manage to keep one foot in the boat.

The Cartography of Rome

Just ten years before the discovery of America, that is at the precise end of the Middle Ages, an obscure — and still unknown — draughtsman produced a panorama of Rome seen from above; from above the Porta Pia. For the first time the physical presentation of the city had been made recognizable, with roofs, houses, towers and monuments almost all in their proper places. This was the beginning of interpreting Rome as history; she seemed to have recaptured her urban reality in this single moment. Thirty years later, the Dutch landscape artist Marteen van Heemskerck was to think of making a detailed and realistic study, from the ground this time, of the most dramatic juxtapositions of ancient and contemporary Rome.

Cartographers began working with an increasingly "scientistic" approach. Examples are Leonardo Bufalini, who published his topographical plan of Rome in 1551, and Giovan Battista Falda, whose 1676 map took in a wide sweep of territory, and includes detail of historical interest.

It was Giovan Battista Nolli from Como who added something really new. It took him twelve years to complete his masterpiece, a relief map of Rome, published in 1748. Nolli's acheivement set a new standard for judging engravings and created a heritage of the topography of Rome that would last till the advent of aerophotogrammetry. Nolli's map influenced a plastic 'panoramic' model made in 1849 by experts in the French Army; only partial, alas, because it was limited to areas of the city strategically important to the French.

Then in 1890, at the same time as the first aerial photos were taken from a balloon, Prof. Rodolfo Lanciani, director of archaeological excavations, began working on a map that is still a reference: The *Form Urbis Romae*, in a 1:1000 scale, permits a simultaneous view of the superimposed strata, the detritus of history, that make up Rome's soil.

Aerial photography continued to develop, but the real coup came in 1912 when Rome was photographed from a very high altitude, with the entire perimeter of the city in view. Only seven years later Umberto Nistri created the first photomap: a complete aerophotographic summary of Rome and its surrounding territory. It was a group started by Nistri, the ETA, that in 1959 produced the third photomap of Rome, one which revealed a city so erratically spread out that the incoherence of its planning could no longer be overlooked: a mushrooming of unauthorized building tolerated, incredibly, for so long.

A photograph from 1928: at the bottom centre are the buildings of the famous "spine of Borgo", a cluster of houses that were to be swept out some years later to make room for Via della Conciliazione and the obelisks arrayed on both sides, like a petrified colour guard.

ANCIENT PLEASURES

After almost 28 centuries, the myth of Romulus and Remus still endures, according to which the she-wolf that graciously suckled the twins provided them with just the right nutritional preparation for the founding of Rome. But why not sketch in another, equally fascinating part of the myth's interpretation?

If we take a momentary leap to the Abruzzi, to the Torlonia Museum in Avezzano, we can have a look at the extremely old relief known as the *Rara Domorum Tecta*, or "Famous Roofs", where there is a depiction of the humble village that, a good 70 years before the Trojan War, Evander and his followers built at the base of the Palatine. There are signs of houses and a couple of larger structures, but what is most striking is the evidence of extensive woods. Could this thicket possibly be the location of that sacred tree the poet speaks of, that guarded the first Romans as a tutelary spirit, and watched over their fates?

It is certain that there were trees, and of more than one kind, even in the Forum: it was said of one giant cypress that fell in Nero's time that it had been there since the years of the foundation (perhaps this was itself the original *arbor sancta*); a lotus spread its root-stock from the Forum Iulium to the city centre; an olive tree and a very leafy fig gave shade to passers-by near the celebrated Pit of Curtius.

As the decades passed, the few trees that survived in the massive construction of roads and temples looked more and more isolated, in the enervating turbulence of the traffic. Commercial, political Rome was a congested place. But phantasmagorical memories of the primordial woods inspired the old Romans to veneration, and then the isolated trees began to take on the look, more and more, of religious sites, circled with a low stone wall or metal fence. Their great age caused them to be seen as the ancient protectors, the generous and understanding gods beloved of agricultural peoples.

Rome expanded, and the noble remains of her oldest habitations had to submit to the humiliation of serving as the footing of new roads for the builders; and blocks of travertine, shining marble, slabs of bronze and ivory piled up on the tufa, the malevolent porous rock the city is made of. With thousands and thousands of tons of stone and metal, Rome learned to build not just patrician villas but cheap housing blocks of three, four and more storeys, to put up colossal temples and statues, great enclosed markets, circuses and public baths.

But in the five and a half centuries of the Republic as in those of the Empire, getting around Rome was anything but easy, because none of the streets, except the very most important ones, had a name. To avoid total confusion and spare immense wastes of time, people inevitably turned to little folk appellations as a toponymic point of reference — traditions that seem to carry an undissipated fragrance from the very oldest days, when the Palatine was still farmland, with addresses like: "I know the house where my friend Caius lives, where the storks' beaks point"; or, "I have to go up the road with the 12 doors"; or, "Sempronia lives at the pomegranate corner."

This was the Rome of streets doubling painfully back on themselves that Augustus Caesar found himself emperor of in the year of his investiture, 27 BC. Forced to rebuild on a day-by-day basis by heaping new layers on top of the old, the metropolis seems to have realized at last that it was turning itself into a malodorous, raucous *souk*. Augustus discovered the indispensable, even urgent solution, needed to revolutionize the city as it neared a population of two million. He reminded his advisors of how, for more than five centuries, the administrative organization imposed by King Servius Tullius had kept the location of houses and public places in a state of paralysis; at the beginning, the city walls had easily contained the four *regiones* of Subura, Esquiliae, Collina (the Quirinal) and Palatium, plus the immemorially sacred Capitoline hill, the cattle market of Forum Boarium, and the Aventine, but there had been an enormous intensification of trade activities, and foreigners settled in the city with their families and possessions, until they made up a quarter of the population. And so it came about that in 7 BC Augustus fixed an administrative reform dividing Rome into not four but 14 *regiones*. A third of these extended beyond the Servian Wall, which enclosed 430 hectares in its 11-kilometre length. At the centrepoint were the tenth *regio*, Palatium, and the eighth, Forum Romanum — the cultural and political heart of the metropolis.

The emperor devised not only territorial reforms, but also reforms of the bureaucracy. A powerful system of high officials came into play: the city *praefectus*, the *curatores*, one to each region, the *praefectus vigilum* heading the fire brigade, and a whole forest of middle-level and small functionaries, from the one charged with the care of temples and public works to those for the aqueducts, the sewers, the conservation of statues.

Ponte Rotto was built in 142 BC by Aemilius Lepidus, and it was a vital link between the heavily travelled Aurelia Vetus and the centre of Rome. The Tiber has battered its powerful buttresses many times; the last, in 1598, reduced this marble masterwork on five pilasters to a single span. Ponte Palatino dates from 1887. Like its less fortunate twin, this bridge is extremely useful in bringing together Trastevere and the heart of the city.

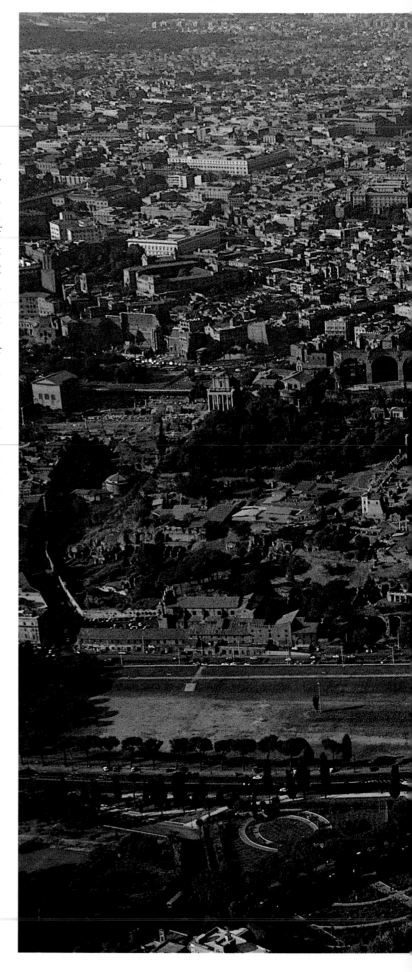

At the centre of the picture is the Colosseum, or, rather, the remaining third of that famous theatre-circus built by Vespasian and Titus on the side of the Domus Aurea lake. As to where the other two-thirds went, one might look for an answer to the materials from which many still-prestigious palazzi and churches were made.

Even as he delighted in having created a body of specialists, Augustus never imagined that he had brought new power centres into being, to intrigue against authority, and to become eventually centres of parasitic corruption.

All this happened to a city in a worrisome state of expansion – dynamic, no doubt, and optimistic, and yet frustrated by the expanding list of restrictions, including those touching on public morality, with which the rich classes were protected. There were considerable social inequities, as the evidence of housing especially shows. It was more or less the same phenomenon as in any metropolis of our time. Augustan Rome had 50,000 buildings of more than one storey, the *insulae*, beehives of cramped rented lodgings, as against 2,000 luxury houses.

Elbow to elbow with each other, the two opposed classes mirrored all the contradictions of their time, and eloquently: the names of the witnesses, anyway, are illustrious. From Martial to Juvenal, Persius, Cicero, Ulpian, a picture emerges of a Rome of two bases, one weighed down by their own triumphant marbles, the other pushed ever closer to a kind of caveman's life.

The gaudy and provocative refinements of the "lifestyle" displayed by the proprietor of a *domus* on the Palatine or Caelius were like a declaration of war to the wretched crowd clumped together in their garrets every evening in heaps of more than three families to a room, or in shop basements, or even under bridges.

The nighttime travelling companions in the multistorey *insulae* were cockroaches, bedbugs and rats. Washing facilities and heating were entirely unknown, because in spite of the abundant water brought into the city on 14 aqueducts, the vital liquid could not reach the higher floors; the technique for sending it there had not been discovered, so there were no water closets, and refuse was often thrown out the windows, with disastrous results for public health and for the heads of passers-by.

On the other side the *domus* and *villae* of the wealthy were equipped with everything; it was like a sacred commandment of the upper caste that the lives of the landed and their guests should be serene, and, inspired by Greek graciousness, that the party should go on. And it did, from the *triclinia* upon which mobs of dinner guests reclined to the Greek-origin peristyle that suffused the house with delightful light, the *cubicula*, bedchambers with their white mosaics, and heating systems that sent warm air through the interstices between the walls.

Since the hovels surrounding it were cleared to make way for the splendid Via dell'Impero, the exedra of Mercati Traiani (Trajan's Market) gives the effect of being utterly detached from the antiquities of the nearby forum. At its shoulders rises the thirteenth-century Torre delle Milizie, an outpost on the long straight way of Via Nazionale, which comes to an end amidst the charms of the Fountain of the Naiads.

Owning slaves was a requisite, if only to affirm status, for a well-to-do family. The slave, in the hellish early years of Rome, was thought of as a thing, which one could dispose of as one wished, with impunity: buy or sell at any time, beat and even kill; their children were slaves from birth, and any that tried to escape could end up crucified or fed to the wild beasts of the arenas.

Later, in the relatively enlightened imperial times, the legislators recognized slaves as having some human qualities and needs: they were permitted to marry, and their children allowed to associate with the master's children, they could buy their freedom for a redemption fee, and as freedmen aspire to respectable jobs as secretaries, farmers, and even teachers. One of Nero's tutors, for instance, was a groom who had been a slave only a few years earlier.

Almost every day, on a revolving platform in the Forum, the market in live humanity went on in open air. The stars were the slave-merchants, *venalicii*; under the supervision of a magistrate, the *aedile*, they presented their astonishingly varied repertory of people in chains: athletic prisoners of war, children and young women captured by pirates and well cared for, as worth their weight in gold, debt-slaves, cooks, dancing girls and learned men imported from the eastern part of the empire. A purchase could affect the city's culture, as in the case reported by Pliny the Elder of a grammarian, bought in the Forum for a fortune of 700,000 *sesterces*.

And even though the more humane of reformers eagerly debated the injustice of such a world, slaves were the mainstay of a social condition of much decorum and dignity. A frugal man like Horace still wanted slaves around him when he was at table, and called his friend Tigellius a miser and a spendthrift because he kept sometimes ten slaves and sometimes 200. Indeed, if we are to believe the scholar Athenaeus, who attended the most splendid banquets of his time, there were some intemperate Romans who owned between 8,000 and 20,000 slaves, many of them of course confined to the latifundia, breaking stones for the construction of new villas and in the evening, bone-weary, herding themselves into the disease-ridden sleeping quarters known as an *ergastolum*.

The contrast between the two planks of Roman society took on sizeable dimensions in the essential aspect of nutrition. The Romans were abstemious, by ancient custom (it is known that their ancestors lived mainly on *puls*, a grain-and-legume porridge, beans, lentils and chickpeas,

and for animal protein, tiny fish pickled in brine); but they had learned to use the pleasures of the table as the favourite way of affirming social success. Eating became the basis of new divisions, starting with the daily bread (*panis candidus* for the rich, refined and snow white, while the poor ate *panis sordidus*, black, of flour that was left over from sifting). The wealthy had their own vegetables (artichokes and asparagus), their own meats (flamingo, peacock, stork and crane), their own fish (sturgeon, mullet, turbot, and of course oysters). Appetites seemed to increase of a sudden when, amid the fearful din, a little wooden sculpture of Greek derivation appeared among the changing courses: the representation of a corpse in the coffin, inscribed, "Drink and be merry as you look on him, for you will be the same when you are dead."

Certain expressions originating at the power centres had unexpected influences: "*Pecunia non olet* (money has no smell)" was not just the emperor Vespasian's reply to opponents of the taxes he levied to pay for the new public lavatories, but turned out to be an entire life-programme — make your living any way you can. And something of the *non olet* must have remained, for centuries, in the people's innermost soul, if a sonnet of Giuseppe Gioacchino Belli, from 1831, is an indication. The poem is *La Madre Der Borsaroletto* (The Pickpocket's Mother): "*Io gliel'ho detto a Checco mio, fijo rubba un mijone e pe'le chiese sarai san Checco e t'arzeranno un gijo.*" (I told my Checco, son, steal a million and the churches will call you Saint Checco and dedicate lilies to you.)

The clouds of urban hypertrophy broke over the people of Rome in a devastating rain. Heaped together in spite of internal divisions in a sea of stone, marble, brick and bronze, the citizens had a very great deal of free time. They were careful not to die as pygmies beneath the enormous feet of the emperors' marmoreal monuments, and they took to emphasizing, more and more, the hedonistic sides of daily life. Women, especially, broke down historic barriers, going out alone, accompanying their husbands to banquets, cultivating with no limits whatever the latest fashions. When short hair was out and blonde and auburn were in, they fought over barbarians' locks and fake hairpieces, as Martial records of the time of the Flavian emperors. As far as that goes, even the men of the period, eaten up by vanity, competed tirelessly over hairstyles, to the point of spending hours and hours with their personal *tonsores*. And these barbers charged extortionate rates,

following the haircut with a curling-iron treatment and perfuming their customers with oceans of floral extracts that, they claimed, no one else could obtain.

Mornings, the Romans ran to the theatre, fascinated by the latest stage-sets and obsessed in their identification with the plots. The *fabulae togatae* and *fabulae praetextae*, comedies and tragedies on Roman subjects, had replaced the foreign shows of earlier times, the Etruscan actors, the Fescennine verses with their popular flavour and scurrilous scenes of everyday life.

The public always wanted more from the actor, wanted to be genuinely moved — to the point of demanding the star's physical death, if it was written in the script! This demand was actually heard in the theatres of Pompey (built 55 BC), of Cornelius Balbo (13 BC) and that of Augusts' son-in-law Marcellus. It was the same collective cry, the same telluric roar that reverberated from the ramparts of the circus. They were shouting in the Flavian Amphitheatre, or as it was — and still is — improperly called, the Colosseum, because it was built on the site where the Colossus of the Sun had stood before it. The debut of the grand massacre — 5,000 animals slaughtered in a hair-raising series of *venationes*, hunts — came in 80 AD, in the reign of the emperor Titus. We can scarcely imagine the joy of the public of 50,000 spectators, but we have evidence of that of emperor Claudius, a passionate fan of the wild beast combats (bear against buffalo, rhinoceros versus elephant) and gladiatorial battles. This tyrant would let the most urgent state business wait from dawn to dusk in order not to miss his appointment at the Flavian Amphitheatre, there to pass sentence, with his famous thumb down (the wounded gladiator had to die) or thumb up (he was to be freed), on the outcome of the fight.

Thumbs were naturally unnecessary in the case of the *scena ad bestias*, a torture invented by Augustus, because the poor soul pushed into the arena had no chance of duelling even for a moment with the starved tigers, lions, and bears that ambled there. The victims of the slaughter *ad bestias* were especially Christians, until the last decades of the fourth century, when the new vision of life propagated by Christianity annulled with a single blow the last cruel survivals of the empire.

And this is where the golden age of classical Rome comes to an end, with the roar of one hungry lion pacing alone on the sands of a useless amphitheatre, already overgrown with brambles.

Vibrant with the symbolism of its design, the Triumphal Arch of Septimius Severus speaks of the devotion of old Rome's people to the emperor and his sons Caracalla and Geta. The arch, completed in AD 203, functions as an esthetic synthesis of the emperor's political contribution to society of the time, ensuring that none of his military achievements are forgotten.

"The Colosseum looked especially beautiful [by full moon]. It is closed at night ...
some beggars have made themselves at home in the crumbling vaults. They had built a
fire on the level ground and a gentle breeze had driven the smoke into the arena so that
the lower parts of the ruins were veiled and only the huge masses above loomed out of
the darkness. We stood at the railings and watched ... By degrees the smoke escaped
through holes and crannies, and in the moonlight it looked like fog. It was a marvellous
sight. This is the kind of illumination by which to see the Pantheon, the Capitol, the
square in front of St. Peter's ..." (Goethe, Italian Journey, 2 February 1787)

Banalized by history clear down to the indignity of souvenir-shop reproductions, the Colosseum is still the world's greatest monument. It took the Flavian emperors 100,000 cubic metres of travertine marble and 300 tons of iron to construct it.

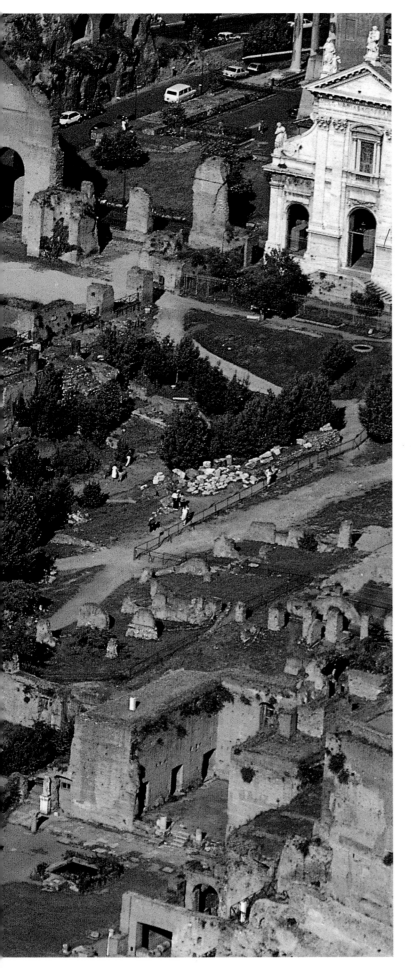

Left: *It took six years of exhausting labour (from AD 306 to 312) to realize what was to be the Colosseum's only rival for magnificence: the basilica of Maxentius. Today, this is a venue for important concerts.*

Above: *Madame de Staël wrote of the Roman Forum (Foro Romano): "No trace remains of the famous tribune from which the Roman people were governed by eloquence, but there are still three columns of a temple raised by Augustus to Jove, and there is a triumphal arch to Septimius Severus. Further, the ruins of a temple dedicated to the Sun and the Moon, constructed for the emperor Hadrian …"*

Among these imposing ruins, where every summer the resounding ritual of the lyric
opera renews itself, Hippolyte Taine passed more than a century ago. "Thus one
arrives at the Baths of Caracalla, the greatest thing to be admired in Rome after the
Colosseum. A human work so deformed by time and events as to appear the work of
nature. Before these arches, vaulted like those of a great bridge, before these crumbling
mounds of masonry, one wonders whether this was not an entire city. There are
1,600 seats of polished marble, the pool is 120 yards long, the dressing room is 80 feet
high, and all this was clothed in the loveliest marble …"

The ruins of Hardian's villa are located not far from the town of Tivoli. This huge collection of buildings is evocative of the places and architectural works which impressed the emperor when he was on one of his journeys to the Orient.

Tivoli is a place full of history and folklore, not as famous as it deserves to be, perhaps for the perverse reason that it is so near the capital. With its hot springs, mountains of travertine (of which a great part of Rome was built) and Villa d'Este amid its gardens and joyous fountains, this town continues to display its rich simplicity, and to lend its name to some of the loveliest parks and meeting-points of Europe and America.

Whether in its Antica or Nuova manifestation, the Via Appia gives fluidity to the capital. The old road was built in 312 BC by the consul Appius Claudius, and it linked Rome to southern Italy. On the left page, the top picture is Hadrian's villa, which is at the feet of Tivoli, while the bottom one is of the tomb of Cecilia Metella, one of the more famous of the tombs and graves which line the Via Appia Antica. On this page are two examples of the kinds of ruins which are found along the Passeggiata Archeologica (Archeological Promenade) sector of the Via Appia.

Porta Metronia is thought to have been a significant site of commercial activity in ancient Rome. Even today its location seems to preserve a continuity between the operative logistics of buying and selling in those days and in the present.

The Pyramid of Caius Cestius (Piramide Cestia) had been hemmed by the Aurelian Walls until the last war, when it was left standing after heavy aerial bombardment brought down part of the walls. This pyramid was erected in just 330 days in 20 BC as the tomb of the tribune Caius Cestius Epulo. A few metres away is the Protestant cemetery, where Shelley and Keats were buried, and directly in front (in the picture) is Porta San Paolo.

THE IDEAL CITY

It seems pointless to rehash the old question as to whether the expression of artistic and philosophical thought in the Middle Ages should be considered "inferior" to the glorious innovations of the Renaissance; all the same, one cannot deny the point made by the eminent historian Chabod, on the differences between the two epochs: "The Medieval man never dared to formulate as a life-ideal, as a theoretical norm, what Leon Battista Alberti was to express in the mid-fifteenth century, proposing the *dolcezza* of living as an ideal." The real substance of the Renaissance "revolution" is comprehensively given in this definition, which we would make nowadays in terms of our concern for the "quality of life".

And what place has a better claim than Rome to being at its origin? Because it was precisely here, where so many ancient masterworks lay buried, that people thought of the exciting idea of seeking one's mirror image in the classical era, the only time a form of idealized beauty had ever been realized.

Thus, at Rome, one May day in 1506, out of the ruins of the Baths of Titus, the Hellenistic sculpture group of the Laocoon came to light; and the attendant outcry echoed in high places. Pope Julius II immediately invited Giuliano da Sangallo and Michelangelo to the site, before anybody knew what statue it was.

Giuliano's son Francesco recalled: "I went down to where the statues were and my father told me right away: this is the Laocoon Pliny mentioned. They widened the hole so that they could haul it out ... and they talked constantly about ancient things."

The first objective for the masters of the 1500s was happily free of stylistic compromise. Above all, it was to recreate the aesthetic model provided by Pliny and Cicero. They both told of a painter of antiquity, the Greek Zeuxis, commissioned to make a portrait of Helen for the city of Crotons, who took as his model not one but five girls, combining the prettiest features of each into a single ideal picture.

The maturing of the Renaissance revival of the classic rules of beauty came with the works of the very great artists of the middle Renaissance — Leonardo, Raphael, Michelangelo. And while these new and vigorous lights began to burn in the artistic firmament of Rome, how far did the city's human reality match their glory, and what new ideals did the ordinary Romans reach for?

In fact, Romans had understood for some decades that there was something new at the gates. Their city was calling them, after the dark years of imperial decline and invasions, to take part once again in the pleasures of prestige and grandeur. The splendid life of the papal court cast its reflections on the rest of the population, leading them into complicit carefreeness, with their respect paid only to artistic innovation, and to strong individualism.

It also meant the rebirth of good living in the sense of an *ars amandi*. A document has been discovered in the Vallicellian Library that suggests a new, more relaxed evaluation of women: "The courtesan or lady of easy virtue not lacking in cultural refinement, is precious to men for relaxation, satisfaction and the cultivation of the qualities of statesmanship." In any case it was that cultivated prelate Ludovico Beccadelli, author of a *Life* of Petrarch, who wrote at the time that "courtesans render greater service to the world than nuns". Let those be merry who will, for who knows what comes tomorrow ...

Thus the maxim of being merry cancelled out all the squalid and fatuous moments of daily life; transforming them into an heedless existence, a freedom that was the finest amusement society offered. Rome and the Church were in this sense akin to each other: to the point where many who had lived openly as courtesans had the posthumous pleasure (no doubt thanks to conspicuous generosity in their tithe-giving) of being buried in very luxurious tombs: Fiametta, Guilia Campana, Penelope, Tullia d'Aragona and Beatrice Spagnola buried in the church of Sant'Agostino; the supremely lovely Imeria, whom the banker Agostino Chigi loved to desperation, the model for a famous nude of Raphael's, buried in the church of San Gregorio al Celio. Another famous *hetaera* of the era, Beatrice de Bonis, known as the Ferrarese, has come down to us dauntlessly through the centuries in undiminished charm, thanks to Raphael, who brought all her graces together for his portrait of "La Fornarina".

And what can one say of the courtesan Lucrezia de Clarice (nicknamed Matremanonvole — "my mother does not want" — because her mother, in the same line, had advised her to answer seducers with a refusal when she was barely 12 years old)? She held a literary salon in her house and argued with no less than Bembo himself.

Traffickers in love held a significant place even in the papal account-books, being vexed from time to time with special taxes for the construction of churches and

And ecco! Paternal, glorious, the great dome of St. Peter's contends with the infinite. The Romans have always called it "cuppolone", dwelling on the "p"s to express how extraordinary it is: if only for its height of 132 metres, including the cross, and its length of 211 metres (the next biggest basilica, St. Paul's in London, is a mere 158 metres).

The mausoleum of the emperor Hadrian, better known now as Castel Sant'Angelo, dates back to AD 139, and it looks very much like a big drum on the banks of the Tiber. Its startling structure and superb location made it world-famous in a different way — as the stage set for two acts of Giacomo Puccini's opera Tosca.

roads; a handy tool for the city administrators, since there was a very considerable number of such ladies. The *Descriptio Urbis* preserved in the British Museum in London records that in 1524 the prostitutes residing in Rome numbered approximately ten per cent of the population of around 55,000. Vanozza Cattanei herself, mother of Cesare and Lucrezia Borgia, had, as a gift from their father Rodrigo, later Pope Alexander VI, a house maintaining three courtesans, with a professional insignia of a red embroidered pillow.

But one German visitor, the Augustinian monk Martin Luther, did not like this Rome in the least — he did not regard it at all as a return to the classical cult of good living. "Bembo, a most learned man, after careful observation of Rome, called it the sewer of the entire world. And one writer said: 'Here all is permitted, except being honest. Examples of religious and worldly ribaldry spill out of Rome like a tide of wickedness ...' Farewell, dear Rome. Let the stinking continue to stink and the sordid still be sordid. If there is a hell, then Rome is built over it."

But not everything Luther noticed in Rome was the target of his execration. In another recollection, like the first from 1510, he actually praised Pope Julius II, "the last drop of oil in a dying lamp" (though he also charged him with an excessive love for material things), and commented positively on the cleanliness of the city, and its orderly policing. But then, in tones of wild invective, he resumes his harangue:

"Too many indulgences for St. Peter's, still in the chaotic stages of its construction; seven years of indulgence for climbing 38 steps of the basilica; get rid of the rope you display as the one Judas used to hang himself, it is a fraud; it is a scandal that the monument of Pope Joan still stands; selling indulgences in Rome for the building of the Vatican palace is simony." And hence: "Let the pope, whose riches are today crasser than those of the richest Crassus, build the basilica of St. Peter with his own money, rather than that of the poor faithful."

But this Pope Julius remained unaware of the fury of the monk of Eisleben. On 18 April 1506, standing beside Donato Bramante, who had built the architectural jewel known as the Tempietto di San Pietro in Montorio on the Janiculum in 1503, he had blessed the laying of the first stone for the new basilica of St. Peter's in the Vatican. The works were so difficult that it was not possible to even talk of completion until the mid-seventeenth century, after

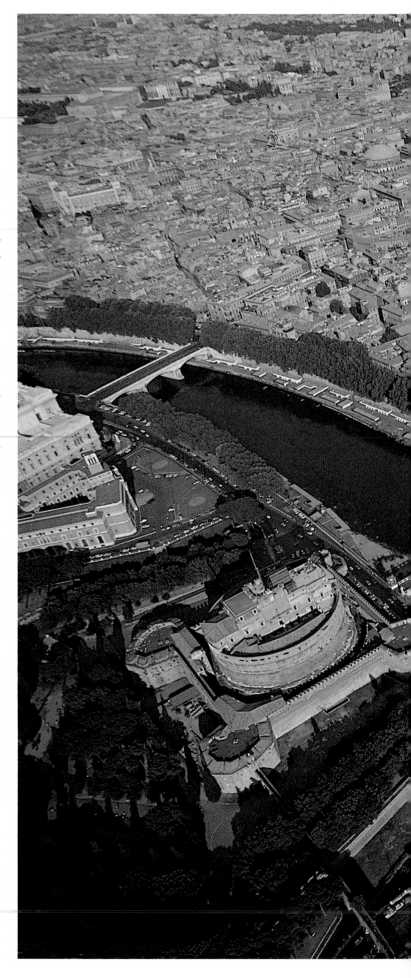

numerous revisions and alterations of the plan.

The pope and his principle artist passed from the scene, barely a year apart, in 1513 and 1514 respectively (Julius to his uncompleted tomb, and Bramante home to Florence), and one pair was inevitably replaced by another: Leo X, son of Lorenzo the Magnificent and Rafaello Sanzio, then 31 years old but already very famous.

To the general disappointment of all, the great energy of the previous pair was not duplicated. Yet Raphael was far from idle, frantically painting in the Stanze and Loggia of the Vatican. But no foreman called him from the worksite of the basilica. Construction had halted entirely. This pontiff it would appear was more content to embellish what had already been built, letting the new church remain undefined, little more than a projected space on the city map. And the "divine" Raphael followed suit. He engaged his architectural genius in the construction of Villa Madama in Monte Mario, the church of Sant' Eligio in Via Giulia, Palazzo Caffarelli-Vidoni, his own house in the Palazzo dei Convertendi, which Bramante had designed years earlier, and Cappella Chigi in Santa Maria del Popolo.

The time of Julius II and the two Medici popes, Leo X and Clement VII (died 1534) saw ambitious new initiatives in the years that followed. The first of them, as an addition to the great basilica, Raphael, Michelangelo, Baldasarre Peruzzi and Sansovino contributed to plans for a great church almost opposite from St. Peter's on this side of the Tiber, to be called San Giovanni dei Fiorentini, and located at the corner of Via Giulia, in a neighborhood where many Tuscans lived. The second initiative involved the reconstruction of the palace at the epicentre of the quarter of Sant'Eustachio, seat of the Medici family and now of the Senate of the Republic. This building functioned as a magnet, drawing the Roman patricians around it: among those who erected their *palazzi* there were the Cenci, the Massimi, the Della Valle, the Leroy. The third initiative was supervised by Raphael and Antonio da Sangallo, and inspired by Leo X: the opening of the Via Leonina (now broken into Via Ripetta and Via della Scorfa) to unite Palazzo Madama to Piazza del Popolo on a 200-metre axis.

The idea of an "administrative axis" also won the enthusiasm of Clement VII, who gave his name to Via Clementina, the 900-meter trajectory linking Piazza del Popolo to Via Capo le Case. The street still exists, but under the name of Via del Babuino. These were also the years in which the idea of the hills as panoramic fortresses took hold, and up went the Colonna's Villa Grimani, Villa Carpi and Villa Albani on the summit and declivities of the Quirinal hill, and on the Palatine rose the villas of the Capranica and Mattei families.

And the design, beyond its indisputable rewards for the landscape, was valuable as well in representing a rational dislocation of the power centre. The same happened in the genuine historic heart of the city, with the building of the Farnese Palace (until the mid-1700s second only to the papal court in cultural and political importance).

All these changes were subject to the independent judgment of the *magistri viarum*, especially under Paul III. It was their duty to oppose individual initiative, thus creating more rational arrangements compared to those that characterized the demolitions of the time of Julius II.

All for himself and his Farnese relatives, Pope Paul III saw in 1539 the completion of a fabulous country residence, the Horti Farnesiani, on the Palatine. From here there are views of the Forum below and up to the Capitol, next to which he had built the four-sided Torre Paolina (torn down 350 years later to make room for the pallid monument to Victor Emmanuel II). Paul loved the Capitoline hill to the point of commissioning the infallible genius of Michelangelo to redesign it entirely. He was so convinced by this great artist that he further charged him to do whatever was necessary to finish the works of the basilica, and *fabricca di San Pietro* has become a proverbial expression to refer to work that is never finished. In short, the era of Paul III was one of great urban renewal, as confirmed by the work in Borgo, Ponte, Campio Marzio, the Aventine and the Bastione Ardentino. During his pontificate there were a total of 450 demolitions of homes to create straight avenues, corresponding to the removal from their homes of 2,000 persons.

The pictures Guido Alberto Rossi has shot of the areas where the Renaissance popes tampered look like the canvasses of a copyist of very great diligence in the matter of balancing positive and negative spaces; but canvases missing, after so much "cleansing" destruction, the special tone of the original urban creation, unplanned, inexorably promiscuous, a topsy-turvy agglomeration where, all the same, the march of time and the affairs of humanity have left a mark, the humble and yet proud antithesis of the geometrical plans that power has stuck on the surface.

*No more than 400 metres from the Tiber, and a couple of kilometres from the Vatican
as the crow flies, Villa Giulia in its gilded isolation calls up the dolce far niente
ambience demanded by Pope Julius III for his country residence. Ammannati
also left some attractive nude female sculptures, which testify to the rather
naturalistic faith of that pontiff.*

Left: *Dominating this side of the Tiber, known as Prati del Castello, is Calderini's bulky white Palace of Justice. It stands ponderously heavy two paces from the spongy banks of the river. The Romans have never accepted this travertine warship, and call it, disdainfully, "er Palazzaccio".*

Above: *The imposing mausoleum of Augustus, wherein rest the remains of the emperor and his family, has almost disappeared from the classical Roman landscape. Like many early buildings, it was used as a stone quarry, and later as a tannery. The final touch was given by Mussolini's urban planners with their "Enlarge! Renovate! Rejuvenate!" mentality — it became a theatre and concert-hall.*

From the dark woods of the Villa Borghese, a few hundred metres from the disturbing Via Veneto, emerges the track of Piazza di Siena, traditional and privileged venue of military celebrations and the most important international riding events.

On the grounds that so enchanted Charles VIII, Annibale Lippi built a grand villa for the Cardinal Ricci di Montepulciano in 1544. Later the building passed into the hands of the Medici, and then France: Napoleon ordered that the Académie Française be installed there, in the Medici Villa as it was known.

The Porta San Pancrazio (at the bottom of the photograph) is ennobled by its proximity to Villa Pamphili and the Janiculum hill. It was in this area that Garibaldi repulsed a French attack, and he set up his headquarters atop these bastions so as to observe the movements of General Oudinot's army in the Revolution of 1849.

An architectural jewel set in Rome's largest public park, Villa Doria-Pamphili is located 300 metres from Porta San Pancrazio. This marriage between art and greenery provides an elegant setting for high-level meetings between dignitaries of the Italian State and other nations.

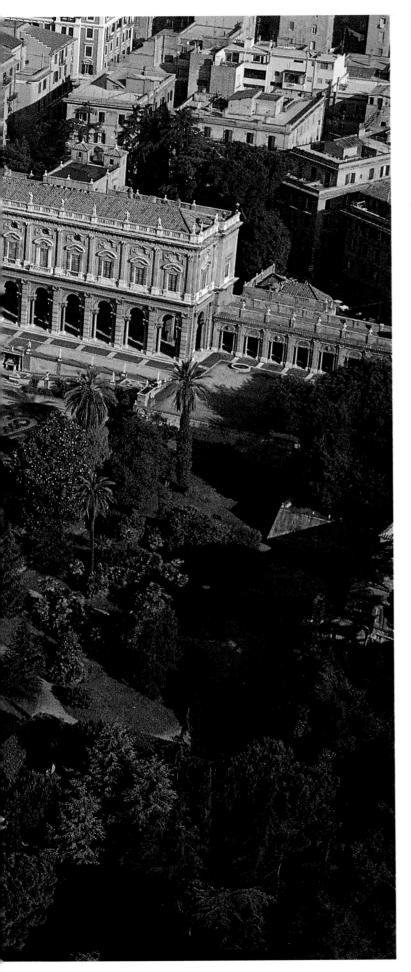

The Villa Albani was built in 1763 by Carlo Marchionni on a commission from Cardinal Alessandro Albani. The architect envisioned a villa divided into three parts: in the centre an Italian garden with the colonnaded villa on the northwest slope and an exedra with a pavilion facing it on the opposite slope; to the left in the picture is the wooded garden, and on the right are the orchards and vineyards. Rome's greatest cartographer Giovan Battista Nolli, Albani's close friend, catalogued 127 villas in those years, 99 of them were within the city walls.

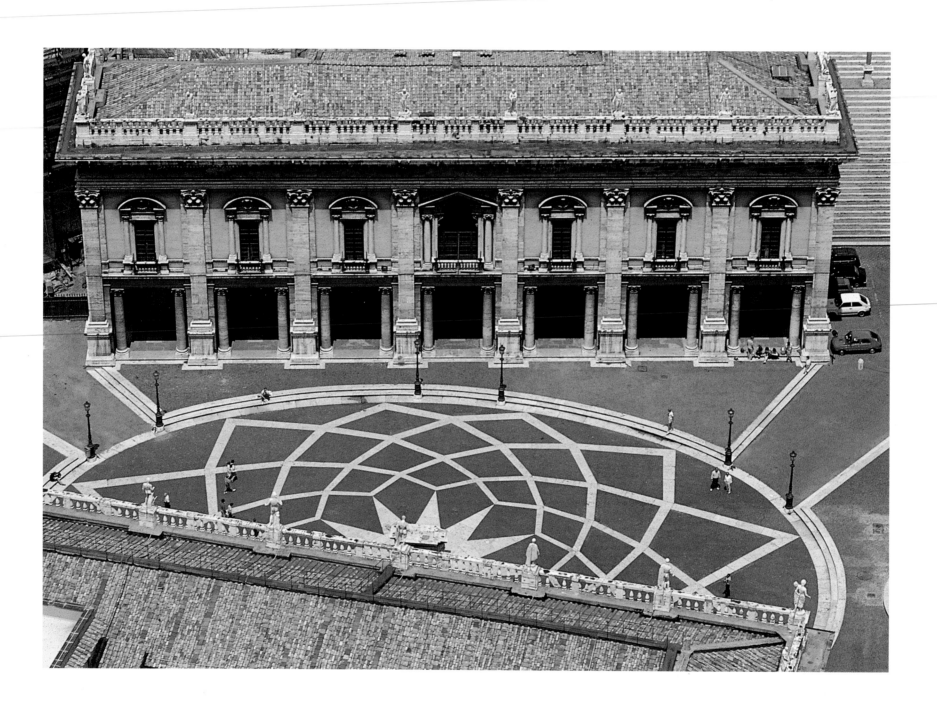

It was on this very hill, the Capitoline (once called the Mount of Saturn), that the Renaissance ideal of reviving and restoring the glories of antiquity and welding them into the new age was realized by Michelangelo. He first designed the geometric pattern on the pavement and set the statue of Marcus Aurelius, the sole remaining example of equestrian statues of the Roman Imperial period, in the centre of the piazza. Then he redesigned the existing buildings and the area around it.

"In general," Charles de Brosses wrote, "the most beautiful part of Rome is its fountains, to my taste. That of Piazza Navona is what has struck me most. Imagine, in the middle of the piazza, this mass of rocks riddled through with holes, and those four rivers pouring torrents of water, and on top a granite obelisk that you must raise your head in order to see ..." He was referring to Bernini's Fountain of the Four Rivers; the others in the square are the Fountain of the Moor and the Fountain of Neptune.

This is also the piazza, more than any other, where you can enjoy the true character of the old-stock civis — in the arrow-swift riposte. This thrust-and-parrying has been going on for centuries, perhaps even in its earliest years when this square was known as the stadium of Domitian, or in the time of Innocent X, when his volatile, intemperate sister-in-law Olympia was the personality of the day. A more lasting example of this trait is the Fountain of the Four Rivers and the church of Sant'Agnese in Agone, material evidence of the Bernini–Borromini "duel".

TWO ARTISTS, ONE STYLE

"Thus Rome has a sixth of the population of Paris and a seventh that of London ...It has neither ships, nor factories, nor commerce. It is true that from the times of Julius II and Leo X until the middle of the last century Rome was at the centre of the fine arts, but it was soon equalled in some and surpassed in others by our capital ... The vaunted palaces are not all equally beautiful and are badly maintained; the larger part of the private dwellings are wretched ... The city, swarming with churches and convents, is almost deserted in the east and south ... It has been said, with justice, that the seven hills of Rome, once the glory of the city, are now only its tomb."

This epitaphical definition, taken from Diderot's *Encyclopedie*, written around the middle of the eighteenth century, opens the book *Roma Barocca*, by Paolo Portoghesi, known worldwide for his profoundly researched studies of that period. And Portoghesi continues:

"In its icy polemic, this definition from the *Encyclopedie* contains, together with many exaggerations, some deep truth. From the time of its fifteenth-century rebirth, the city of the popes had become continuously more of a theatre-state, a kind of gigantic historical spectacle in which a heterogeneous population performed its daily comedy without having the cohesion or political strength to form a real community ... fatalistically awaiting the succession of popes as the only concrete possibility of change."

One may want to characterize the period from 1650 to 1750 as one which attempted to overturn classicist myth. If so, it is impossible to escape the the architectural formulation of this upheaval. It was an architecture well-suited to the demands of the theatre-state, and a style that many later critized for its excesses. The Baroque style was, in Portoghesi's words, the "institution of a new compositional method, which broadens and transforms the classical repertory into the promise of thrilling new discoveries through a new conception of space."

And, one might add, of time. The time it took urban architects and reformers to give life to the long link roads set real records. Indeed 25 years passed from the commencement of work on the Via Ripetta to the definition of the Via Condottie, and the same from the first modernization of Strada Pia to the inauguration of Strada Felice. The whole was executed on the basis of a papal master plan prepared with magnificent openness (considering the carnage visited on numerous preexisting works).

This approach, as implemented by popes from Nicholas V (1447–55) to Pius VI (1775–99), under the pretext of annihilating medieval Rome, built first Renaissance and finally Baroque Rome. The birth of the new city signalled the affirmation of a "vital vision of human experience, as a continuum of potential movement in which stasis is only a fugitive interval". This dynamicism yields happy moments, which must be captured, whatever the cost.

Gianlorenzo Bernini briefly summarized the inspirations of his sculpture: "The most beautiful moment for the mouth is either when it stops speaking or when it starts." And again, "One of the most important points is to have a good eye for judging contrasts, because they do not just appear as they are but also in relation to what is near them — a relationship which changes their appearance." Finding his ideal travelling companions, the natural elements to work with him toward the achievement of his goal, was not difficult for Bernini, who was to have a hand in so many projects in the city of Rome.

Literally fascinated by the spectacle of water ("the waters do much good to my soul") he invented the metallic holes in the railings of the Ponte Sant'Angelo so that the pedestrian can admire the flow of the Tiber below. The Roman travertine, mined in the hills of Tivoli, goes well with the intuitions of the artist, who saw unthinkable vibrations in its rough porosity and specklings of mold-green and volcanic-mud brown — vibrations, in this case, felt by those of modest means as well as by cultivated aristocrats, since the language of the Baroque, here, in Rome, asserts a culture of the whole citizenry. The city-dwellers participated in these urban spaces, and still do: an architectural achievement that urban planners of our era have never been able to match.

Bernini himself provided the confirmation when he wrote: "If anyone in Rome is unjust, it is not, at any rate the public." They had taken up unreservedly whatever was revolutionary in the new architectural standard of men like Bernini and Borromini: the discovery of the quality of space, as opposed to line, and the resolutions that discovery entails. They prodigally produced dynamic perspectives that had never been seen before. This was the era when it was possible for an observer to appreciate fully, from every single angle, the architectonics behind the new conception of the city.

Now that Romans are beginning to enjoy their city again, they speak of a visual culture of the Baroque. The

The chromatic descent of the Roman sunset on the dome of San Carlo al Corso seems intended to give an emphasis to the Church's influence in the heart of worldy, commercial Rome represented a mere step away by a great Corso hotel, and opposite by the jubilant Via Condotti.

Twilight is an enchanted hour for St. Peter's Square and the sacred buildings; silence and solitude return after the stressful throngs of the day depart. At this magical moment between day and night, before the city twinkles to life with night's lights, the priests charged with the pastoral care of the pilgrims catch their breath in solemn reflection and prayer.

credit goes to a small squad of geniuses. Michelangelo, for instance, had established in the Capitol and Saint Peter's centres of interest and visual attraction with an authentically organized spatiality, with depths of perspective, which went beyond the closed and somewhat austere stasis of Renaissance classicism.

The urban reforms of those years deepened the intentions and desires expressed by Rome's powerful patrons, the popes. From the Church's need for a tangible sign of proselytism followed its visible demonstration, with the lines that joined one basilica to another: pagaents of endlessly majestic processions that hypnotized, in particular, the rich foreign pilgrims.

As it painted its face in the new urban style, Rome was getting dressed triumphally for the Counterreformation. The *primo assoluto* of this show was Gianlorenzo Bernini. From Paul V to Gregory XV, from Urban VIII (his greatest protector) to Innocent X (who preferred Borromini, at one time), from Alexander VII to Clement X, all these popes had commissions for Gianlorenzo, a passionate and many-sided artist, in conformity to the highest ideals of artistic achievement in the seventeenth century.

Nevertheless Bernini had one great sorrow — his failure as a painter to equal Caravaggio, the artist from Bergamo who died in 1610, and whose work was greatly admired in, precisely, Rome, in the churches of San Luigi de' Francesi and Santa Maria del Popolo. Bernini certainly shared with Caravaggio the idea that art should represent, above all, the subject's spontaneous expression.

But his sculpture and building design could not take second place to distractions among the paintbrushes. His greatest project, the colonnade of Saint Peter's, permitted him to introduce an unparallelled novelty: the 284 Tuscan columns provide multiple changing views, between the exterior and the interior of the elliptical movement. The colonnade symbolizes the inevitable integration between Church and city. It is an embrace and a perpetual dialogue conceived by the master of the Baroque for the Mother of the Church "so as to show how maternally she receives with open arms the Catholics, to confirm them in their belief; the Heretics, to return them to the Church; and the Infidels, to illuminate them in the true faith," as he himself described the dramatic logic of the colonnade's encompassing of Saint Peter's Square.

Within Saint Peter's are other masterworks of Bernini as architect and sculptor, the completion of a triumph:

the Baldachin (an ornamental canopy) over Saint Peter's tomb, ordered by Urban VIII, the Barberini, the majestic Throne of Saint Peter for Alexander VII, the funeral monument to Urban VIII, the Ecstasy of Saint Teresa, the Scala Regia. In Paris, 15 October 1665, when they tried to retain him to construct the Louvre, he replied, "I must go, I have certain children in Rome that I cannot bring to Paris, the Throne of Saint Peter, the Colonnade ..."

In the seventeenth century all Rome was plunged into the rivalry between Bernini and Borromini, deriving immense artistic benefits from it. While the first was an extrovert with a predilection for the dramatic and grandiose and a penchant for important materials — bronze, marble, travertine — the second, more of an intimist as we would say today, closer to the rigorous life of the monastic orders and to the essence of early Christianity, preferred simple materials, bricks and plaster, exalting them all the same with his overflowing talent. Borromini's works were planned to be the memorial, in the future, of a maturer Christianity. His quest was utterly anti-monumental.

Borromini did not match his great rival for longevity: Bernini died in 1680, while Borromini had a tragic end on 12 August 1667, when, overcome by a nervous crisis, he took his life with a sword. His professional progress, his works in opposition to those of Bernini, shook the city and divided it into two parties. The polemics became more and more fiery and his supporters even went to the point of repeating, at every streetcorner, the story that he and not Bernini had made the Baldachin of Saint Peter.

Borromini's legacy of art to the city of Rome speaks eloquently of his worth: from the cloister and church of Saint Carlo to the Quattro Fontane, to the Oratory of the Filippini, to Sant'Ivo alla Sapienza, with its little spiral lantern, to the modernization of San Giovanni in Laterano, to the church of Sant'Agnese in Agone, to Piazza Navona, to the bell tower of Sant'Andrea delle Fratte, to the church of Santa Lucia in Selci, to the Palazzo di Spagna, to the colonnaded perspective of Palazzo Spada, a true illusionist masterpiece. Borromini's facade for the College of the Propagation of the Faith was to be widely studied, and imitated, by lesser architects of the Rococo.

Pietro da Cortona, Carlo Rainaldi, Alessandro Algardi, and Carlo Fontana are among the architects and sculptors who left other incisive works in the churches and on the *piazzas* of Baroque Rome. Carlo Maderno established public acceptance of the new style with his facade of Santa Susanna, though he will probably be better remembered for the facade and nave of Saint Peter's.

The end result of this creative efflorescence was a city that is ringed by a conspicuous number of streets, laid out in the name of Baroque artistic expression; the streets are those that leave from Piazza del Popolo in the form of a trident (Ripetta, the Corso, Babuino), then run into Piazza di Spagna and Via Condotti, and then from Via Sistina to Santa Maria Maggiore. The last of these arteries had been ordered by Sixtus V in 1585, a pope who still exercises a singular influence in the Roman memory, and not only for having entrusted a man like Domenico Fontana with the urban reconstruction of Rome (leading to the Aqueduct of Aqua Felice, the Borgo Felice, the obelisk in Saint Peter's Square and the completion of the dome of Saint Peter's) but also for his inflexible temperament, to which compromise was foreign.

It is said of this pope, who was also, in accordance with the tastes of the time, a bit of a fortune-teller, that having learned of a crucifix that gushed with blood, he dashed into the church where it was happening and, before a crowd of dismayed believers, smashed the symbol of the divine sacrifice, crying out: "As Christ I venerate you, as wood I cleave you asunder!"

And it is certain that he was right, since he had guessed intuitively that the sacristan, by way of collecting some pennies from the gullible among his congregation, had hidden a sponge soaked with red-coloured water in the wood of the crucifix. And it is from that day that the folk rhyme has circulated that Romans use on someone whose scepticism goes too far:

"Papa Sisto
   Pardons no one,
      Not even Christo."

It is, after all, an act of faith in the intransigence required of Big Bosses; and also in men whose feet are set firmly on the ground, determined to be respected.

We learn more of this from another catchphrase of the time, applicable to those Romans for ever relegated to the second division: *Ommini, bisommini e cazzabubboli* (ordinary men, superior men, and men of no account, or generally on the *gonzo* side). This *cazzabubboli*, so Roman in its rotund onomatopoeia, was the one with which those mediocre imitators of Bernini and Borromini were branded, in the eighteenth century, when their mannered "baroquisms" insulted the churches and palaces of Rome.

It took the popes Paul III, Pius V and Urban VIII a good century (from 1534 to 1644) to fortify the walls of the Vatican. But most memorable is the pontiff Leo IV, who in 851 first took on the task of building these walls. They defined what is still known as the "Leonine City".

Perspective of the basilica of St. Peter: the dome, which together with the apse represents Michelangelo's work on the building, dominates the foreground; the Via della Conciliazione stretches beyond the square, Castel Sant'Angelo marking its end-point. Beyond it is the white Palace of Justice.

The Berninian embrace —
Bernini's majestic colonnade
of St. Peter's Square —
gives the effect of gathering
up the multitudes to the
bosom of the Church. In the
centre of the square, there is
an Egyptian obelisk taken
from Nero's circus,
crowned with a cross. This
obelisk was brought to Rome
in AD 37 under the orders
of the emperor Caligula.

At these twilights of amber reflection all visitors, without exception, feel a certain closeness towards one another. It suddenly becomes a love-debt rolling down from the Trinità de' Monti to its beloved, the Via Condotti, there at its feet — a discreet rivulet that looks narrower than it actually is.

From the sixteenth-century
facade by Carlo Maderno,
the church seems to request
that embrace called for by
Pope Sixtus V between the
two poles of Christianity so
dear to him: Santa Maria
Maggiore and Santa Maria
del Popolo. Meanwhile
down Fontana's staircase in
front, the later centuries
have shipped in a multitude
of artists, aesthetes and,
today, clients of all
nationalities dazzled by
boutique displays and
jewellers' windows.

Still gathering on the Spanish Steps, it seems, are the same "types" who huddled on its porous stone divans in the days of novelist Charles Dickens. "The first time I landed there I could not account for why these faces seemed so familiar to me. After a time I realized that I had contemplated them, over the course of a number of years, in the canvases of various Expositions. There, for instance, is the old gentleman with the extremely long white hair; ... the classical model of the worshipper, or the patriarch. This other, pretending to have fallen asleep in the sunshine ... is the model of the dolce far niente ..."

Always classified as the famous transition point between Rome's industrial zones, the Piazza del Popolo is watched over by the twin churches of Santa Maria de Montesanto and Santa Maria dei Miracoli. The strategic location of the two churches makes them voluble witnesses of the explosions of happiness — often quite dramatic — that are to be found in this piazza when a Roman team gains a great sporting victory.

The Corso (Via del Corso) was once called Via Lata (Broad Street), but no one could have imagined that it would become a sort of European Fifth Avenue for its importance, length and tasteful architecture. The buildings of this street may be thought of as the strategic bastions of Rome's historic centre.

It was mid-seventeenth-century architect Carlo Rainaldi's idea to "twin" the two churches (Santa Maria de Montesanto and Santa Maria dei Miracoli). This was meant to confer a majestic solemnity on the urban renewal which was then beginning in Rome. While the churches are the brainchild of Carlo Rainaldi, artists from Sansovino, Bramante and Raphael to Manetti, Bernini and Valadier have left their mark on and in them.

83

Not too rich in historical references, the shady avenue known as Corso Vittorio
Emanuele II is often "utilized" for logistic reasons by those who make a daily mark
in politics and business. Its layout as we see it today dates to the decade of the
1880s, and one can see the unfortunate disembowelling of the city's
districts as they stood in Renaissance times.

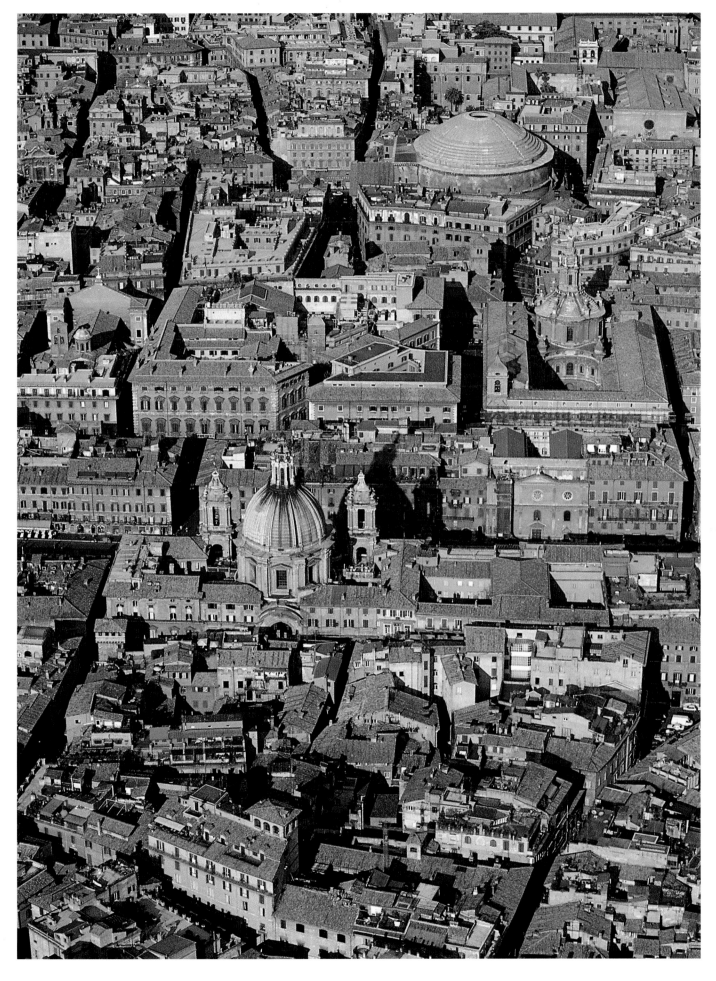

With all the demolition and development ordered under the various regulatory plans produced since the end of the nineteenth century, this area of the old wards of Ponte, Regola and Parione no longer recalls much of its old Renaissance design. The unique survivors are some hundreds of little hole-in-the-wall shops — precious homes for the traditional inventiveness of the Roman artisan class.

Above: *From on high the fountain of Piazza della Rotonda can be compared to a table centrepiece, a piece of marvellously light lace. It was built in 1575 by Giacomo Della Porta, with help from Filippo Barigioni and Vincenzo Felici (they did the statues), under the patronage of Pope Clement XI.*
Right: *The Pantheon dominates with its majestic roundness. This temple to the gods was built by Marcus Agrippa, and it was later turned into a church. Raphael was buried here. The building with a baroque facade to the left of the Pantheon is Palazzo Madama. It was erected in 1500 by the Medici, and was some time later the house of Margaret of Austria. Today it is the Senate of the Republic.*

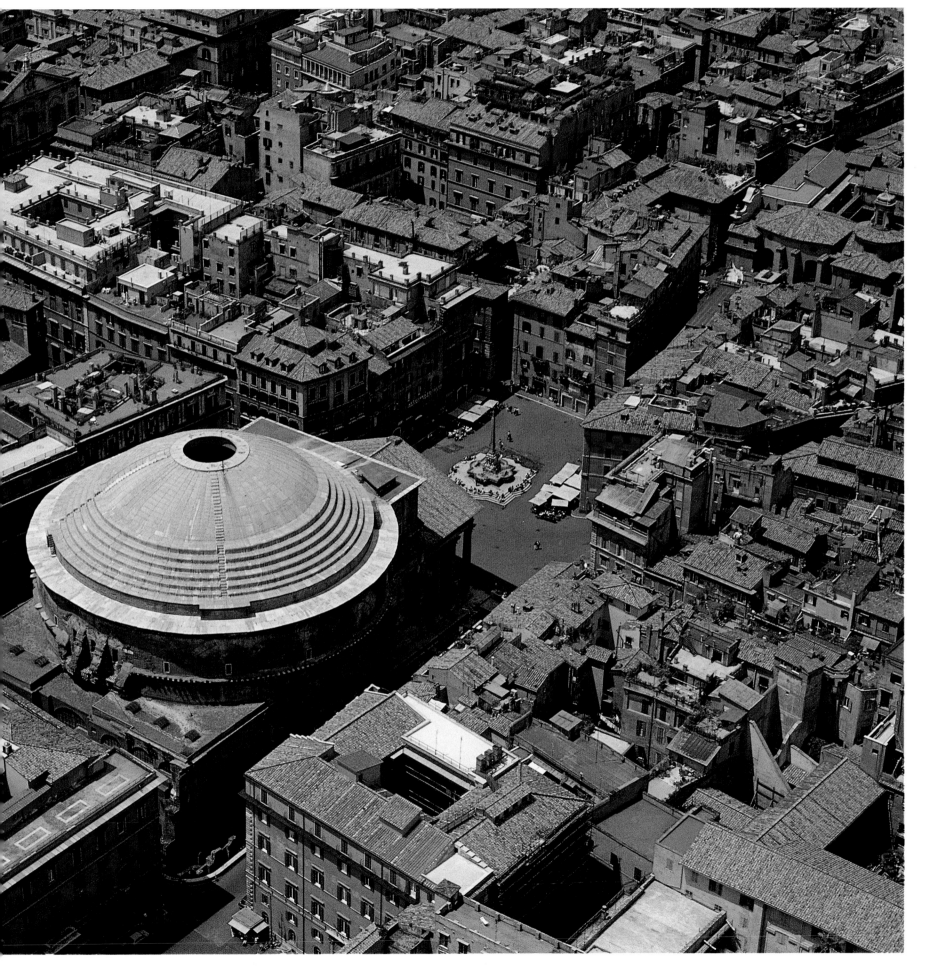

The fountain called "La Barcaccia", in Piazza di Spagna, is almost as well-known internationally as Trevi. Built in 1629, its design is attributed to Pietro Bernini, father of the famous Gianlorenzo. For more than two centuries artists and models have chosen it as the preferred spot for their appointments, and now there is no foreign visitor who will not wish to sit down here for at least half an hour, for, if nothing else, it is the best place to admire the great staircase of Trinità de' Monti (the Spanish Steps).

A splendid choreography in stone, Nicola Salvi's Trevi Fountain has won, since its birth in 1762, the admiration of all visitors. Built for Pope Clement XII, this fountain is carved out of one side of the palace of the dukes of Poli. Salvi wrote that the fountain was to signify "the immense visible mass of the sea which, dashing again and again as it falls against the rocks, leaps back into the air, dissolves into white foam and then flows once more ..."

The "inconvenient" nearness of the basilica of Maxentius has not prevented Santa Francesca Romana from gaining a little notoriety. In fact, preserved in this church are two stones upon which Saint Peter knelt while delivering the oration that brought about the downfall of Simon Magus (Simon the Magician).

A see-saw of terraces and television antennas in the Trionfale quarter at the foot
of Monte Mario: day and night the banners of the new media break the silent
rhythm of this most modest neighbourhood.

Once the opponents of royal power liked to refer to this ample space as "the king's private garden". Today, the presence of the head of state makes the "garden" (Quirinal Palace) a meeting place on the Republic's national day (on 2 June) for personalities from the worlds of the arts, labour and politics.

The hill, product of a long accumulation of detritus and classical ruins, is tied to the beginnings of the city's political life. Its Latin name Mons Citorius recalls the elections that took place here over 2,000 years ago. Today the Chamber of Deputies sits on Montecitorio. The building was commissioned by Pope Innocent X for the solemnization of his niece's marriage to Prince Ludovisi. Since he wanted something magniloquent, the pope engaged Bernini to be both the architect and the sculptor.

Rome's National Museum, located in a sort of cloister behind Piazza Esedra, is no more than a kilometre from the chaotic Stazione Termini. In the deafening traffic noise, restorers and archivists work to systematize the immense store of finds from various archeological sites, as well as chance discoveries like the extraordinary fresco from the house of Augustus' wife, Livia, or the celebrated throne of Ludovisus.

The Tiberina isle was formed by alluvial deposits. Its tenth-century church of San Bartolomeo has some connection with the Templars. This island was the site of a temple of Aesculapius, the god of medicine, and of a hospice for the old and sick.

Although Porta Pia is not steeped in history the way many other more ancient gates are, this gate, constructed between 1561 and 1565 to replace Porta Nomentana, enjoys great popularity. It was through this gate that the Italian troops entered Rome on 20 September 1870 after the French withdrew from the city; this was the beginning of a unified Italy — and the origin of the myth of the "Breach of Porta Pia".

*The two belltowers of the side facade of San Giovanni in Laterano (St. John Lateran)
face an Egyptian obelisk. Built of red granite this is the first of Rome's 13 obelisks,
and it is the tallest, at 31 metres 47 centimetres. To the right of the obelisk is the
Bapistery of St. John, a fourth-century building and one of the earliest Christian
buildings with a circular ground plan.*

The church of San Pietro in Carcere is on the north side of the Roman Forum. It forms a refuge from the tumultuous traffic of Via dei Fori Imperiali, which can be glimpsed at the top of the picture.

Here is another demonstration of how the Church attempted to impose itself on past epochs, especially during the eighteenth and nineteenth centuries. This little church rises over the vestiges of the classic world, in the form of the Forum of Trajan. Ironically, the even more imposing Vittoriano now dominates this area.

In the first half of the fourth century, Pope Liberius informed the faithful that the Virgin had instructed him to build a church on the Esquiline hill, where snow had fallen in August. The church was to be called, simply, Santa Maria della Neve (Santa Maria of the Snow) …

Today the basilica of Santa Maria Maggiore (founded in 432) rules over the hill with
matronly assurance, but it is well charged with memories, some tragic. It was here that
the books of the heretics were burned; the rebels of Ursinus were stoned by order of
Pope Damascus; and Cola di Rienzi was crowned emperor.

More than 15 centuries old, Santa Maria Maggiore, the fourth patriarchal basilica of Rome, has always held art treasures as well as incredibly valuable gems. The most memorable of them all, to date, is Arnolfo di Cambio's sculpture of the Manger, part of which is now housed in the Sistine Chapel in the Vatican.

THE *DOLCE VITA*

Rome and her palazzi, Rome and her traffic, Rome and the Pope, and so on … Using commonplaces to stereotype a city with an evolution reckoned in millennia seems ungenerous and disloyal, like railing at an old lady who no longer has the will or the means to defend herself, or offspring to do it for her. Apparently there is not a sufficient reserve of fanaticism in the majority of the Roman population — for more than half a century it has given up its heart, *er core* in the city dialect, to the adaptive talents of the capital's two football teams, FC Roma and FC Lazio. The clubs are to be "blamed" for channelling, on alternate Sundays, the emotions, the sensitivities, and unfortunately the aggressions of an average of 40,000 people, whose greatest wish is to be imprisoned in the Olympic Stadium. Whether it is a chance phenomenon or not, contemporary Rome's relation to sports is a good illustration of her stubborn but positive "lightness of soul".

The metropolis has become something like one of those seaports of the New York type, a megastructure sectioned into infernal circles, like Dante's hell, ready to receive whatever or whoever comes. Visions of this city bring strangers by the thousands, to discover something to do, to take any bit part on life's stage, to invent or improvise the same things that, as it happens, provided daily bread for the Romans of 200 years ago. True, the street stall, the ice cream cart, the on-the-spot artisan are all international realities. But only Rome is a universal frame that gathers in and gives a home to these simultaneously rich and poor moments, soaked in sentiment.

The central train station, Stazione Termini, is the crossroads for the *pendolari* (the pendulum people, as they call those who leave the capital every day at dawn for a job 100 kilometres away), but it is also, and to an even greater extent, a strongbox of melancholy, an unfair salad of failed plans, education taken halfway and unresolved utopias. The mood runs through an entire chromatic scale, but the tendency is toward what the psychoanalysts call "the tonality of the sad disposition".

All this may sound as if it is introducing a marked pessimism, but establishing a cinematographic kind of contrast turns out to be very useful for a better understanding of the whys and wherefores of contemporary Rome.

A capital fragrant with politics, and the worldliness of the *Dolce Vita* that Federico Fellini celebrated in the '60s now, thanks to the economic recovery, appears to be flourishing once again. But that is also the triumph of its own history, a history that has led to the definition of Rome as the city of double sovereignty.

The shadow of ambiguity, given substance by the temporal power of the papacy, has caused the city to split into two mutually dependent atoms — in a sort of communicating vessel of power. And power, as always, shows its negative valences as well as its positive ones.

It has been said, more than once, that management on the basis of the positive elements only would trigger an inflation of banalities, those commonplace expressions of "Romeness" referred to earlier on. The negative moments, on the other hand, are beautiful and imbued with suffering, in violent contrast to the tranquility a situation of reciprocal domination should impose. But talking of "power", there is no need to end the discussion with the marriage between Rome and the pope.

Much of Rome's energy and dominance stems from the visual impact that still comes across to those who live in the city. The revision of an architecture of glory goes back to the 1870s, and the projects to construct buildings to launch the "sensation of power" for the capital of a new nation, are now firmly preserved.

Under the ministerial direction of Quintino Sella, when Luigi Pianciani was the mayor, the structures that were to make Rome into a highly functional administrative centre were built. And all sorts of ecclesiastical buildings were requisitioned by the state, destined to be the defensive bulwarks of the Roman bureaucracy.

Then came the turn of the Tiber, a historical river for perhaps too many reasons. At this point, it could no longer be considered in its ulterior strategic role, as a last-gasp defensive bulwark, and so the plan was to build new bridges, to provide a more fluid link between parts of the city that had once been sealed off from each other. Out of reverence, and also for convenience's sake, the key logistic arteries were christened with the high-sounding names of royalty — Vittorio Emanuele, Umberto, Margherita — as well as of the personages that had led people to a serious understanding of what a *patria* might mean, Giuseppe Garibaldi or Camillo Benso, the Count Cavour.

Decades later, well into the twentieth century, the urban order had to come to terms with the historical force of fascism. A reflexive kind of nostalgia for imperial *Romanitas* won out over the architectural good taste of the beginning of the century, and painted Benito Mussolini's

This "glass palace" is the embodiment of a great industrial enterprise. Similar in certain respects to the United Nations headquarters in New York, the ENI building seems to control the flow of commercial activity in the surrounding area.

Monochrome and architecturally invasive, the Palazzo dei Congressi, ordered by Mussolini for the world exposition of 1942 (which was never held), affirms the tendency of the time to break with the traditional forms. It is now one of the symbols of the "city-satellite" of EUR.

monolithic pretentiousness in disturbing white. Thus began an endless series of works in the "lictorial" style, with its marble scrolls and faces. The EUR district, which is still productive, went up in 1942, planned as the venue for a world's fair. Clearly, power once again played an influential role on a civilization under domination. Rome became a city in waiting, for the eventual awakening of a new era based on dictatorship and colonization.

In the postwar period Rome reacted with ill-tempered vigour, a true heritage of the people that shifted the Colosseum's 100,000 cubic metres of travertine into place.

But the workers were paid less generously, at the time. And then, a unique combination of circumstances produced the economic boom, and Rome was, for the first time in her history, a place of cheer, of well being, productivity and unrestrained optimism.

Through his lense, Fellini was able to capture all of the wealth and beauty of the *Dolce Vita* myth. Via Vittorio Veneto, like a Champs Elysèes to the south of Paris, provided an open-air society salon, winter and summer. Anything Rome had to offer, from cinema to heavy industry and from fashion to sport, had to start by obtaining the *placet*, the approval, of the crowd on Via Veneto. A kind of healthy madness was the order of the day, comparable with the reassuring memory of the imperial feats of Augustus, or his surrogates. One could hardly deny that the emperors enjoyed their amusements.

"It was all so easy!" recall the *palazzinari* — the developers — of those days, who helped build what was considered to lie on the outskirts of Rome, developments that have now come to squeeze the historical centre of the city. The writer Guido Piovene, who thought of defining today's Rome as a "peculiar conglomerate mineral" was not far wrong. The idea of an architectural, ethnic, and commercial potpourri allows for the coexistence of a patrimonial image of the ancient city — an eternal testimony in an eternally sealed envelope.

To conclude, it would be an empty rhetorical flourish to insist on the spiritual presence of the many, no, the too many people that have ennobled Rome, or been ennobled by her. People of great qualities: simplicity and the perfectly innocent indolence that has allowed the city to sleep through so many thankless moments. It may be that, in the mind of the reader, the visitor, she will remain Rome and her palaces, Rome and her traffic, Rome and her pope …But that wouldn't be her fault.

The headquarters of the Food and Agricultural Organization (FAO) of the United Nations is at the end of Passeggiata Archeologica and the Palatine hill. It makes up part of the landscape of the EUR quarter, an area originally set aside to house the Roman World Exhibition that was never held because of the outbreak of the Second World War.

The Palace of Labour (Palazzo della Civiltà del Lavoro) in the EUR looks as if it is planned as a symbol of the continual plagiarizing of the old Romans' beloved arches. But as the years pass, it becomes clear that its true nature is to be a handy geometric backdrop for fashion photography or automobile expositions.

It can now be said that the EUR residential complex has turned out to be the only really functional satellite town of Rome, even if surviving buildings from the Fascist period, with their awkward solemnity, may cause the residents a bit of embarrassment.

The relaxed character of the Romans protects them from finding in the nascent chaos of the traffic a source of pathological anxiety. The blocco, or jam, shown here, in the San Giovanni zone, represents the normal condition of at least 14 out of 24 hours. For the driver in this snarl, calm resignation is the mode: work can wait.

The bridge was built to unsnarl the traffic which overflowed around the residential area near the Vatican and to send it to the commercial centre beyond the Tiber. Its construction entailed the destruction of the useful gate, the Porta de Ripetta. Named after Count Carvour, this bridge, the seventh of the Roman bridges, has united the Prati quarter with the Corso since 1902.

In 1988 in the course of an investigation for Venerdì, the weekly magazine of La Repubblica, journalist Paolo Guzzanti wrote: "Around the Stazione Termini, today there grows a mysterious city, ethnically uncertain. Men who do not know what to do lean for hours and hours against parked cars ... Every day pullmans arrive full of Polish exiles, shivering babies, baskets and suitcases. Something reminiscent of New York at the beginning of the century ..."

In 1574 this was the only entrance to Rome from the Via Appia Nuova; today it stands as one of the symbols of a city bent on economizing. Indeed, a little to the left, Via Sannio can just be seen — part flea market and part "jeanseria", but not quite in the class of the notorious Porta Portese.

119

Ondina, Oceania, Nereide and Naïade: these names stood out in the scandal of the Fountain of the Naiads in Piazza Esedra, constructed by Rutelli in 1901. At that time the four tableaux vivants, with their truly inviting nude bodies, had divided the city into two parties: for or against these "speaking" nudes? To our good fortune the "sì"s had it, and the four florid models from Anticoli (the village of Ciociaria that furnished these and so many other graces to the artists of the time) still stand there with their bold joie de vivre, smiling day and night at the tourists who disembark at the Stazione Termini near by.

An ancient column,
a dogma (that of the
Immaculate Conception),
a date for celebrating it
(8 December 1856) —
these are the absolutely
inseparable elements
that bring the Catholic
population every year to
Piazza di Spagna to
venerate the Mother of
Christ, and the current
pontiff.

It looks like a trick played by the anti-Roman league, if there were one, pitting houses barely a century old against the ancient city across the Tiber. All the same, the tireless urban planners that transformed the countryside of Prati del Castello into a squared-up second city actually did a big favour to old Rome — they turned it into a more secret jewel-box, a collage of the new and some extraordinary antique pieces.

This second Rome rose in the Prati after the Piedmontese occupation of 1870, and indeed the new architectural angularity recalls Piedmont's capital of Turin. The quarter confronts the surviving Renaissance and Baroque residences of the historic centre, so that the Palace of Justice, a funereal box of pallid enormity, insolently squares off against Via Zanardelli and Piazza Navona.

In the heart of the Jewish district (the Ghetto) are the ruins of Torre Argentina (Silver Tower). Though not proven, it is firmly believed that these ruins stand over the place where Julius Caesar was assassinated. The abandoned landscape suggested this dry epigram to writer Ennio Flaiano: "All these stones, you find them there and don't use them, leave them like the leftovers of a rich dinner-party."

The Via Arenula and Ghetto area represents a subtle marriage between the essentially
Roman way of life and the tastes and customs of the Jewish ghetto. These streets
testify, more than others, to the cruelties of the last war and the Nazi occupation.
Almost ironic is the presence, in Via Arenula, of the current Ministry of Justice.

Perhaps no other public monument, at least in Italy, has been the topic of an ongoing controversy for so many decades. Almost 80 years have passed since the inauguration of this milky monument to King Victor Emmanuel II, the Savoyard who ordered the occupation of papal Rome on 20 September 1870 (thus paving the way for a unified Italy), and whose statue now stands, in the form of a bronze warrior, at the centre of the construction.

The "giant inkwell", as some humorists have called it, also earned the sarcasm of the famous director Alfred Hitchcock, on his first visit to Rome. "I'd like to drip, slowly, down those white steps, tons and tons of yellow paint. This, you see, is the true function of the monument: to be transformed into a modern white-and-yellow Vesuvius."

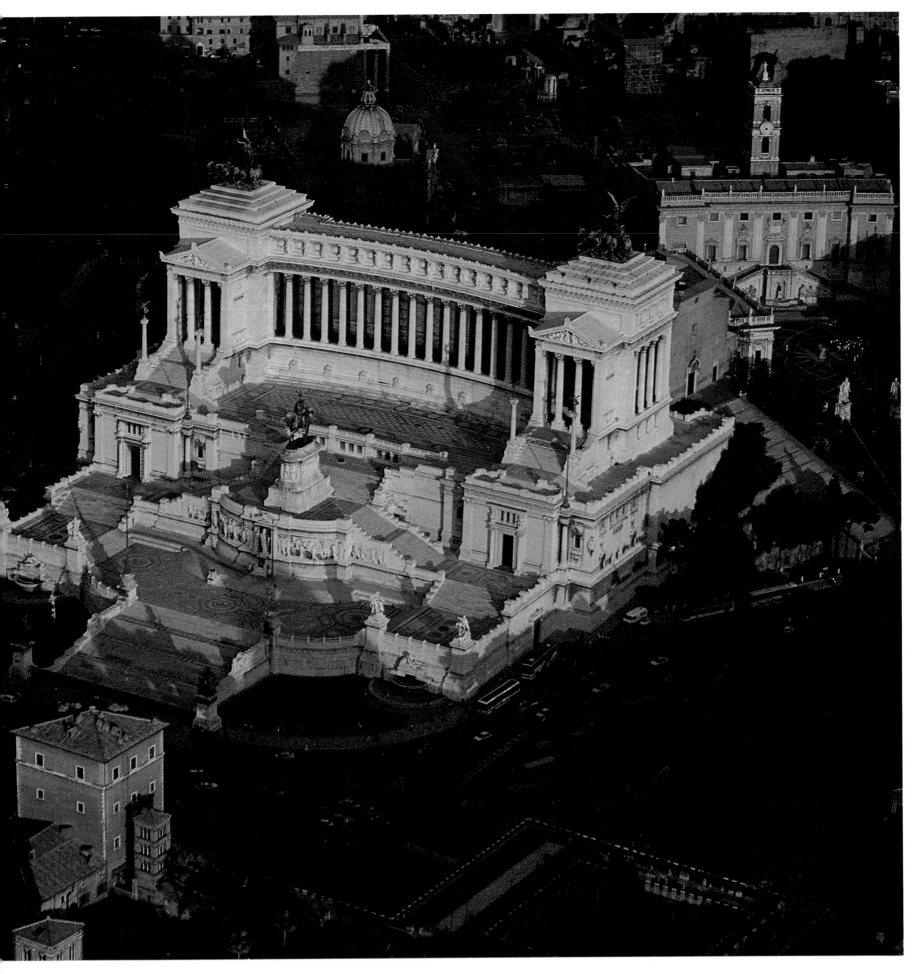

*Imitations of the Augustan era, mosiacized memories, nostalgia in Carrara marble:
the historical hybridization that Fascism spent 20 years trying to inculcate into
Italian youth appears here, herded in the plurisportive space of what was
then Foro Mussolini (now Foro Italico).*

Since 1951, when it was completed, Ponte Flaminio has been a Bridge of Eros. Its
255-metre length is covered with gigantic appeals in multicoloured paints, transfixed
hearts, sighing lips and even the occasional threat. Note: "Nina, my little rabbit, why
don't you come back to me?" — "Tina, you are the most beautiful in the world" —
"Maria, if I leave it's your fault. You'll pay for it!"
Then once a month the city cleaners cover the great messages with whitewash. In vain.
That same night other broken hearts take up their paints …

A circular house, more like a cottage than a shelter for animals, hosts tortoises,
alligators, huge lizards, and coiled serpents obsessively concerned with their changing
skin. It is one of the most pleasing buildings of the Zoological Gardens of Rome, which
date from 1911 and extend 19 hectares behind Villa Borghese. The Zoo shows its
3,000 specimens to an army of visitors every day.

A little over a century ago, interlocking rows of canebreak were annoying obstacles in the gardens here in the Flaminio quarter, then totally rustic. Today the quarter is growing, stretching as it does from Stadio Flaminio to Ponte Milvio, and becoming known as one of the gathering places for Rome's ever-transforming middle-level bourgeoisie.

Left: *The Lungotevere Flaminio, with some of the most exclusive tennis clubs of the capital, is dedicated to Roman relaxation. During the lunch and dinner hours idlers and sportsmen congregate to work off some of the day's tensions before taking the Viale G. Mazzini back to their homes and offices.*
Above: *At the back of the Flaminio quarter are the Foro Italico installations. These were built between 1929 and 1937, and the 1960 Olympic Games were held here.*

Gregory the Great lived here, and hence "his" church was built here, a short distance from Passeggiata Archeologica, where Appius Claudius Caecus began the Queen of Roads — the Via Appia. This place is doubly sacred, the mantle of trees protecting the church are known as a bosco perenne (perpetual wood), blessed, according to popular belief, by heaven.

Dedicated to the martyr Sebastian, killed in 304 under the orders of Emperor Diocletian, this church quickly became an important one, earning the designation of Basilica Apostolorum. Ever since, it has received pilgrimages daily from the faithful from all parts of the world, who marvel to find it nestled in the serene embrace of tall pines of the Via Appia Antica.

A "religion" the people of Rome have always professed: the riposo — a retirement to some exclusive residence sheltered in the greenery of the Castelli Romani, the Aventine, Cassia or Aurelia (pictures from top left downwards). This retreat has often given the literati, the painters and the directors who enjoyed this privilege the opportunity to develop their creative spirits greatly.

Two houses of very different appearance in the Roman campagna: such rustic scenes can be found surprisingly close to the city itself.

Above: *This collection of buildings belongs to the monastery of San Gregorio al Ceilo. It is not far from the Colosseum.*
Page 144: *A final swoop over the monument that says "Rome" — the Colosseum — seems a fitting good-bye to this splendid city.*

INDEX

About, Edmond 22
Alaric 20
Alberic 22
Alberti, Leon Battista 49
Alexander VI (pope) 49
Alexander VII (pope) 68, 70
Algardi, Alexander 70
Ammannati, Bartolomeo 53
Augustus Caesar 27, 97, 110
Barcaccia (fountain) 88
Basilica Apostolorum (church) 137
basilica of Maxentius 38–9, 90
Baths of Caracalla 15, 32. 40
Belli, Giuseppe Gioachine 22
Bembo, Pietro 49
Benso, Camillo 109
Bernini, Gianlorenzo 22, 67, 68, 70, 80, 96
Bernini, Pietro 88
Borgia, Lucrezia 15
Borromini, Francesco 22, 67, 68, 70
Bramante, Donato 22, 50, 52, 80
Brosses, Charles de 64
Calderini 55
Cambio, Arnolfo di 107
Capitole 62–3, 68
Caravaggio 68
Castel Sant'Angelo 48, 50, 72
Cavour Bridge 117
Chabod, Federico 49
Cicero 28, 49
Claudius (emperor) 32
Clement VII (pope) 52
Clement X (pope) 68
Clement XI (pope) 86
Colosseum 8–9, 28, 29, 34–7, 39, 110
Constantine (emperor) 18
Corso Vittorio Emmanuele II 84–5
Dickens, Charles 79
Diocletian (emperor) 137

Eugene IV (pope) 20, 86
EUR (Esposizione Universale di Roma—district) 108,109, 110–5
Falda, Giovan Battista 24
Farnese Palace 52
Fellini, Federico 109, 110
Flaiano, Ennio 20, 124
Fontaine, Carlo 70
Fontaine, Domenico 70
Foro Italico 130, 135
Foro Romano (Roman Forum) 15, 16, 27, 30, 39, 102
Fountain of the Piazza della Rotonda 86
Garibaldi, Giuseppe 58, 109
Genseric 20
Ghetto 15, 125
Goethe, J.W. 15, 22, 35
Goths 18
Gregory XV (pope) 68
Guzzanti, Paolo 118
Hadrian's Tomb (= Castel Sant'Angelo) 22
Hadrian's Villa 41, 45
Humberto I (king of Italy)109
Innocent X (pope) 68
Janiculum 24, 50, 52, 59
John XI (pope) 20
Jules II (pope) 49, 50, 52, 67
Julius Caesar 18, 124
Lanciani, Rodolfo 24
Leo IV (pope) 70
Leo X (pope) 50, 52, 67
Leonardo de Vinci 49
Liberius I (pope) 104
Lippi, Annibale 57
Lombardo, Giovanni Paglia 22
Lungotevere Flaminio 133–5
Lupinacci, Manlio 22
Luther, Martin 49, 50
Maderno, Carlo 70, 77
Marchionni, Carlo 61
Marmorata (port) 16
Marozius 20
Martegani, Ugo 15

Martial 16, 28
mausoleum of Augustus 55
Medici Villa 57, 86
Michelangelo 49, 52, 63, 68
Mussolini, Benito 55, 110
Nero (emperor) 27, 28
Nicholas V (pope) 67
Nistri, Umberto 24
Nolli, Giovan Battista 24, 61
Oudinot, General Nicolas Charles 58
Palazzo Barberini 22
Palazzo dei Congressi 110–1
Palace of Justice 54–5, 72, 123
Palazzo Madama (Senate of the Republic) 52, 86–7
Palazzo Spada 70
Pantheon 8–9, 86–7
Paris, Matthew 24
Passeggiata Archeologica 45, 112
Paul III (pope) 52, 71
Paul V (pope) 68
Peruzzi, Baldassare 52
Petronius 30
Pianciani, Luigi 109
Piazza Esedra 97, 120
Piazza Montecitorio 96
Piazza del Popolo 15, 52, 70, 80-3
Piazza della Rotonda 86–7
Piazza di Spagna 22, 70, 78-9, 88, 121
Piazza Venezia 15, 22, 23
Piazza Navona 22, 64–5, 70, 123
Piovene, Guido 110
Pius V (pope) 70, 71
Pius VI (pope) 67
Ponte Flaminio 131
Ponte Milvio 15, 133
Ponte Palatino 27
Ponte Sant'Angelo 2, 4–5, 67
Pontelli, Baccio 22
Porta Metronia 46

Porta Pia, the myth of 100
Porta del Popolo 7, 24
Porta San Giovanni 119
Porta San Pancrazio 58, 59
Portoghesi, Paolo 67
Prati del Castello (district) 55, 117, 122
Rainaldi, Carlo 70, 83
Raphael 49, 52, 80
Roman National Museum 97
Ronsisvalle, Vanni 15
Ruga, Pietro 24
Rutelli 120
Saint Gregory the Great 136
Saint Peter 90
Saint Peter's (basilica) 22, 25, 49, 50, 52, 68–75
Saint Peter's Square 22, 49, 68–9, 70, 74–5
Salvi, Nicola 89
San Bartolomeo (church) 98
San Carlo al Corso (church) 67
San Giovanni dei Fiorentini (church) 52
San Giovanni in Laterano (Saint John Lateran, church) 70, 101
San Gregorio al Celio (monastery) 49, 142
San Pietro in Montorie (church) 22, 50
San Pietro in Vincoli 102
Sangallo, Giuliano da 49
Sansovino, Jacopo 52, 80
Sant'Agnese in Agone (church) 70
Sant'Agostino (church) 20, 49
Sant'Andrea delle Fratte (church) 70
Santa Francesca Romana (church) 90
Santa Lucia in Selci (church) 70
Santa Maria Maggiore (church) 70, 77, 104–7
Santa Maria dei Miracoli (church) 80

Santa Maria de Montesanto (church) 80
Santa Maria del Popolo (church) 22, 52, 68, 77
Seneca 32
Serge III (pope) 20
Sistine Chapel 107
Sixtus V (pope) 22, 70, 77
Stäel, Madame de 39
Stazione Termini (central railway station) 97, 109, 118, 120
Taine, Hippolyte 40
Tiberina (island) 19, 98–9
Titus (emperor) 28, 32
Tivoli 42–3, 67
Torre Argentina 124
Trajan's Market 30, 103
Trevi Fountain 22, 88, 89
Trinita da Monti (church) 16, 22, 76, 88
Trionfale (district) 91
Triumphal Arch of Septimius Severus 102
Urban VIII (pope) 68, 70
Vasari, Giorgio 49
Vatican City 10–11, 50, 52, 53, 70, 107
Via Appia 18, 44–5, 136–7
Via Arenula 125
Via del Babuino 52, 70
Via Condotti 16, 24, 67, 70, 76
Via del Corso 67, 70, 82
Via Giulia 53
Via Ripetta 15, 52, 67, 70
Victor Emmanuel II (king of Italy) 52, 109, 127
Villa Albani 60–1
Villa Borghese 56, 132
Villa Carafa (Quirinal Palace) 52
Villa Doria-Pamphili 58, 59
Villa Giulia 53
Villa Lante 24, 52
Villa Medici 57
Vittoriano (monument to Victor Emmanuel II) 8, 23, 52, 89, 126–9
Zoological Gardens 132

ACKNOWLEDGEMENTS

The publisher and Guido Alberto Rossi would like to thank the Italian Air Force SMA 2 Reparto for their help. All the photographs have their Permit SMA No. 834 of 18 August 1987. Thanks are also due to pilots Mauro Pompa and Vincenzo Calabrese. The publisher is also indebted to the following for the old materials and photographs: Museo di Roma (engraving, page 19), Musée des plans et réliefs, Paris (model, page 21), Sovrano Ordine Militare di Malta, Rome (photo, page 23) and Ministero dei Beni Culturali (photo, page 25).
Finally, a special thank-you must be said to His Excellency, Mr. Alessandro Vattani, the Italian Ambassador to Singapore, and his wife, Francesca, for their invaluable assistance.

Sources of the quotations:
Belli, G.G.: *I sonetti* (Mondadori Editore)
Flaiano, Ennio: *Una e una notte* (Bompiani Editore)
Goethe, J.W.: *Italian Journey*, trans. W.H. Auden and Elizabeth Mayer
(William Collins & Sons, 1962)
Insolera, Italo: *Roma* (Laterza Editore)
Lupinacci, Manlio: *Qui Roma* (Touring Club Italiano Editore)
Martegani, Ugo e Vanni Ronsisvalle: *Roma, il diavolo e l'acquasanta*
(Canesi Editore)
Petronius: *Satyricon* (De Carlo Editore)
Portoghesi, Paolo: *Roma barocca* (Laterza Editore)